Native American
Religious Action

Studies in Comparative Religion
Frederick M. Denny, *Editor*

The Holy Book in Comparative Perspective
Edited by Frederick M. Denny and Rodney L. Taylor

Dr. Strangegod: On the Symbolic Meaning of Nuclear Weapons
By Ira Chernus

Native American Religious Action: A Performance Approach to Religion
By Sam Gill

Native American Religious Action:

A PERFORMANCE APPROACH TO RELIGION

By Sam Gill

University of South Carolina Press

Published in Columbia, South Carolina, by the University of South Carolina Press

Manufactured in the United States of America

Grateful acknowledgment is made to the following publishers for permission to reprint copyrighted material:

"The Trees Stood Deep Rooted," *Parabola* II:2 (1977): 6–12.
"The Shadow of a Vision Yonder," in *Seeing with a Native Eye: Contributions to the Study of Native American Religion*, ed. by Walter H. Capps (New York: Harper & Row, 1976), pp. 44–57.
"It's Where You Put Your Eyes," *Parabola* IV:4 (1979): 91–97.
"Whirling Logs and Colored Sands" is a revised version of an essay originally published in Earle H. Waugh and K. Dad Prithipaul, eds., *Native Religious Traditions* (Waterloo, Ontario: Wilfrid Laurier University Press, 1979, for the Canadian Corporation for Studies in Religion).
Portions of "Disenchantment: A Religious Abduction" previously published in "Disenchantment," *Parabola* I:3 (1976): 6–13, and in "Hopi Kachina Cult Initiation: The Shocking Beginning to the Hopi's Religious Life," *Journal of the American Academy of Religion* XLV 2, Supplement (June 1977), A: 447–64.
"Prayer as Person: The Navajo Conception of Prayer Acts," *History of Religions* 17:2 (1977): 143–57.
"Nonliterate Traditions and Holy Books: Toward a New Model," in *The Holy Book in Comparative Perspective*, Frederick M. Denny and Rodney L. Taylor, eds. (University of South Carolina Press, 1985) pp. 224–39.

Library of Congress Cataloging-in-Publication Data
Gill, Sam D., 1943–
   Native American religious action.

   (Studies in comparative religion)
   Bibliography: p.
   Includes index.
   1. Indians of North America—Religion and mythology.
2. Indians of North America—Rites and ceremonies.
3. Navajo Indians—Religion and mythology.   4. Hopi
Indians—Religion and mythology.   5. Navajo Indians—
Rites and ceremonies.   6. Hopi Indians—Rites and
ceremonies.   I. Title.   II. Series.
E98.R3G483   1987   299'.78   87–5896
ISBN 0–87249–509–4

For my good friends
DELWIN AND NANCY BROWN

Contents

Editor's Preface   ix

Acknowledgments   xi

Religion by Abduction: An Introduction   3

The Trees Stood Deep Rooted   17

The Shadow of a Vision Yonder   26

"It's Where You Put Your Eyes"   37

Whirling Logs and Colored Sands   47

Disenchantment: A Religious Abduction   58

"And he took away their wings": Story and
    History in American Folk Traditions   76

Prayer as Performance: A Navajo Contribution to
    the Study of Prayer   89

Prayer as Person: The Performative Force in
    Navajo Prayer Acts   113

Holy Book in Nonliterate Traditions: Toward the
    Reinvention of Religion   129

One, Two, Three: The Interpretation of
    Religious Action   147

Good-bye Columbus: An Afterword   173

Bibliography   178

Index   184

Editor's Preface

The comparative study of religion has been known by different names in the century of its existence as an independent field, and it has been pursued both in the humanities and social sciences. This series makes no special claim for the term "comparative religion" beyond viewing it as a widely recognized label for an equally wide range of scholarly interests and approaches. "Studies in Comparative Religion" is a series of books by leading specialists on a variety of religious traditions and topics. The series is committed to viewing religion as a universal dimension of the human condition and the study of religion and religions as an enterprise that can and should be made intelligible beyond narrow disciplinary, area studies or confessional boundaries. Although this series has been planned for optimum accessibility by a broad spectrum of educated readers, each book will also provide either results of new basic research, theories and interpretations, or surveys and discussions of important and enduring issues—or combinations of these two kinds of enterprises.

The first book in the series was *The Holy Book in Comparative Perspective*, co-edited by Rodney L. Taylor and the series editor. It is an example of the second type of project just mentioned. Such a survey is not intended to produce original research, but the contributions by specialists in each tradition can be consulted with confidence as authoritative introductions to religious traditions.

The second book, *Dr. Strangegod: On the Symbolic Meaning of Nuclear Weapons* by Ira Chernus, is an example of the first type of book envisioned for the series. This book strikes out in a radical new direction to analyze nuclear weapons and the arms race in light of modern theories about ultimacy and religious experience, and the genesis as well as maintenance of religious symbols and myths. *Dr. Strangegod* is the first sustained history of religions analysis of nuclear weapons.

The present book, Sam D. Gill's *Native American Religious Action: A Performance Approach to Religion*, is a combination of the two types of books that will mark this series, for it breaks new theoretical ground in the study of Native American religions while at the same time it considers this still embryonic field against the assumptions and traditions of the academic study of religion in general. Gill is a pioneer in the study of Native American religions and his challenging and absorbing chapters, some previously published, have been gathered with a view to providing a sense of the field as it exists at present. In *Native American Religious Action*, then, we see not only the current progress of a new sub-field in religious studies, but also developments in the thinking of one of its formative scholars.

Frederick Mathewson Denny
General Editor
Studies in Comparative Religion

Acknowledgments

The research, writing, and publication of the essays in this volume span more than a decade. Several of the essays appear in print here for the first time. There are many who have contributed to my efforts. Many are the Native Americans, particularly Navajos and Hopis, who have opened their homes, their activities, and their personal lives to me and my family. To them I am deeply grateful. The support, guidance, and encouragement of Alfonso Ortiz and Emory Sekaquaptewa have been essential.

Professor Michael Silverstein has had more influence on this collection than he likely knows. His studies of the pragmatic aspects of language, particularly as expressed in his lecture "Metaforces of Power in Traditional Oratory," have been an inspiration and model for many of the concerns I have had in the study of religion. I want to acknowledge his influence, and also to thank him for his generous support and guidance.

There are several institutions with which I have been affiliated that have supported my work. The Museum of Northern Arizona in Flagstaff was my first research base while still a graduate student at the University of Chicago. It not only provided access to a wonderful library and interested colleagues, it published my first article, invited me to do my first real public lecture, and provided much-needed financial support. Arizona State University, where I taught for eight years, provided numerous research grants and much collegial support. The University of Colorado, Boulder, has provided similar support. I wish to thank Frederick Denny, the general editor of the series in which this collection appears, for his support and Rodney Taylor and Dean Everly Fleischer for their support and enthusiasm about my research and writings.

Some of the articles that appear here for the first time were originally prepared as lectures: "It's Where You Put Your Eyes" at Wichita State University, (1979); "Whirling Logs and Colored Sands" at the University of Alberta (1977); "And he took away their wings" at the University of Kansas and Adrian College (1984); "Good-bye Columbus" at a National Endowment for the Humanities conference in Santa Fe (1983) and "Holy Book in Nonliterate Traditions" at Reed College (1983). My thanks to the many kind hosts and engaging audiences.

I want to thank Kenneth Scott, editor at the University of South Carolina Press, for his critical suggestions, and also Thomas Parkhill, who read many of the essays in the collection with a helpful eye.

I have revised, sometimes extensively, most of the essays that have been previously published in order to make terminology consistent; to expand, clarify, and amplify the intended objectives; and to give emphasis to themes that would provide unity to the collection. Still it is a collection, and was not prepared to stand as a single unified and wholly consistent piece. I certainly hope that my knowledge and insight have developed during the last decade, and I hope that development unfolds throughout the essays in the collection. I appreciate the permission to reprint granted by the original publishers of these articles.

Family and friends are what make life a pleasure. I want to thank Judy, Corbin, and Jennifer for making my life a very happy one. By dedication of this book, I want to express my love and appreciation to Delwin and Nancy Brown. I cannot begin to tell them how much their friendship has meant to me and my family.

Native American
Religious Action

Religion by Abduction:

An Introduction

I will always vividly remember the first time I attended a Hopi kachina dance. My family and I were living on the Navajo reservation at the time. We went to Hopi to see a summer dance called Niman, which is the occasion when kachinas, spirit beings who appear as masked figures, bid farewell to the Hopi people before returning to their homes in the San Francisco Mountains. The kachinas appear at Hopi at the winter solstice and remain until Niman. I knew little about Hopi culture at the time, and its complexity and richness still humble me. Even so, the experience I had was unforgettable. It was one of those transforming experiences, not simply because I was so moved, but because I was confronted with questions and concerns that cannot easily be put aside.

Arriving at Third Mesa we parked our car just outside the village of Hotevilla and started walking the dusty road toward the village. As we neared the village, we could hear somewhere in the distance the sounds, *clack, jingle, clack, jingle.* We did not know the location of the plaza, but soon we saw groups of Hopis hurrying along converging paths. Infected with their anticipation, we picked up our pace. We climbed an ancient ladder to a pueblo rooftop and found ourselves peering into the village plaza. We were scarcely settled when the kachinas entered the sun-drenched plaza through a narrow opening between pueblo houses. They carried green cornstalks and cattails and armloads of fruit, bread, and other goods. Which they put in the center of the plaza. As the figures formed a line around one end and along part of one side of the dance area, I could begin to appreciate the detail of their appearance, so stunningly colorful in contrast with the brown earth of the plaza and the adobe pueblos.

They were *angak'china* or long-hair kachinas, perhaps forty in number and uniform in appearance save their great differences in size. Most distinctly, each had shining long black hair hanging midway to the waist, both in front and back. A turquoise-colored face interrupted the hair in front. The narrow eyes and mouth were rectangular areas of yellow and red. Three downy feathers hung from below the mouth. At the crown of the head was a cluster of yellow downy feathers, and extending upright from the back of the head was a single brilliant macaw feather. A cotton cord hung down the back of the hair, attached at the end to either a bejeweled shell or a small woven plaque. Downy feathers were attached at intervals along the cord. Clay markings decorated the naked upper body. A kilt was worn bound by two sashes, one wide woven cotton one colorfully embroidered near the ends, the other narrow and woven in red, black, and green designs. A fox pelt was attached at the back of the waist, the tail nearly reaching the ground. Spruce boughs adorned the waist. A large turtle-shell rattle was strapped to the right calf and a band of sleighbells to the left. These instruments were the source of the clacking and jingling that foretold the arrival of the kachinas. Turquoise moccasins were worn. A gourd rattle was carried in the right hand and spruce boughs in the left. Each figure was heavy-laden with turquoise jewelry—bracelets, necklaces, and bow-guards.

When all had found their places, a hush fell over the plaza and a figure with massive torso stamped one heel, bringing his turtle-shell rattle to life. Remaining in place he repeated again and again this barely perceptible movement. *Clack, clack, clack,* —the rhythm was quickly taken by the line of dancers. Then, in the same fashion beginning with a lead figure, their song welled up among the group to fill the plaza. The songs were highly melodic yet deeply sonorous, somewhat light in mood yet stately. The songs were accompanied by turtle-shell rattle, sleigh bell, and hand rattle sounds which integrated the dances and the songs.

Verbal descriptions are dull reflections of such events. Not even photographs and sound recordings (neither are allowed) would do justice to the dances. They engage all of the senses, and at least for the Hopi these dances resonate with the whole of Hopi culture and history. Over the years I have attended a number of kachina dances at Hopi, and I have always been fascinated and moved.

While the nature of my experience at a kachina dance contributes nothing to our understanding of Hopi religion, I cannot pretend that it has not been a force in motivating my pursuit of an understanding of the religions of Native Americans. It was an experience that, to my feelings, was undeniably important and laden with meaning, yet I was unable adequately to articulate the importance and meaning I believed to be there. The flood of questions that arose from such experiences has provided much of the agenda for the work I have done. The importance of these experiences and the questions they have posed is reflected in the chapters of this book. I have come to believe that the very nature of such reorienting experiences can stimulate important growth within the academic study of religion.

The academic study of religion has been, and will continue to be, indebted to ethnology, anthropology, and other social sciences. Yet, particularly in light of my experiences at Navajo and Hopi, I have been confounded by why students of religion have so willingly neglected the study of Native American religions and, more widely, the religions of nonliterate, or as I now prefer to say "exclusively oral," peoples the world over. The materials for the study of the religions of these peoples are rich, extensive, and available. The important academic issues and problems to be dealt with are seemingly endless. There is ample evidence of this, for in the history of the Americanist school of study, students of language, folklore, history, and society have made important contributions to the understanding of Native American cultures, and these studies have contributed more widely to the theory and general wisdom of these fields of study.[1] Yet despite the extensive records and current opportunities for study, despite the continuing important work of Americanist studies, despite the interest in Native American religious systems maintained by other fields of study, despite even the widespread popular interest in the area which brings students into the classrooms, the interpretive study of Native American religions has been virtually ignored by the modern academic study of religion. There are very few religion scholars who concentrate their teaching and research on the cultures native to the Americas.[2] There are complex historical reasons for this neglect. I think many of them cannot be separated from the history of Christianity in America. While this is an issue that must be dealt with more fully at another time, the impact it has had on our understanding of religion and our approach to the study of religion must be considered here, and I will do so as I consider another set of issues and questions that stem from my experience observing Hopi ceremonial dances and Navajo curing ceremonials.

As I began to study such complex events as Hopi kachina dances and Navajo ceremonials from the perspective of the academic study of religion, I began to think that my difficulties in interpreting and understanding were linked to the form of the available data. My data were complex sets of cultural objects and actions. Most often I did not even have the actual cultural events available for study, but only descriptions of them, and I have already noted the complexity, yet inadequacy, of such descriptions. There are abundant descriptive and interpretive studies motivated by interests in many aspects of culture. But where religion is a significant part of a study, it is usually as a window into other facets of culture such as the related systems of economic exchange or social and political systems. I was not wanting for data; in fact, I was engulfed by data. But in the terms of my training as a student of religion, I had no text, no canon upon which to base an interpretation of these highly complex yet clearly meaningful events. There is no written history, no dogma, no records, no written philosophy, no holy book. Our usual approaches to the study of religion were largely unusable and inadequate.

Seemingly the options for studying these events are limited. We may—as many have done—seek an explanation from the peoples themselves. We ask them, "Why do you do this?" or "What does this mean?" We then accept as exegetical such statements as "We do this to make rain," or "We do this to turn the sun back in its course," or "We do this so that someone may be cured of an illness." But since these explanations clash with our commonly understood and unquestioned principles of physical cause and effect, we often append to them clauses that exempt us from these seemingly fallacious beliefs. We add such clauses as, "They say . . ." or "They believe . . ." or "They act as if . . . ."

There are several failings of this explanatory approach. First, we misunderstand the nature of the statements we solicit. They are usually as needful of interpretation as the acts and events to which they refer. They are not exegetical in the sense we expect them to be. Second, in accepting such statements as explanation and by not facing the discord they strike with our accepted understanding of causality, we in effect patronize Native Americans. The various faces of patronism, worn often in the guise of humanism, are among the most subtle demons that prevent the advance of understanding and the establishment of intercultural relations. Third, in citing such statements as suitable explanation we simply dismiss the full detail of these extraordinarily complex events. While we acknowledge that all of the details may matter to them, we resolve that these do not matter to us beyond presenting as accurate and as objective a description as possible.

Pursuing an alternative approach to understanding, one that gives attention to the details of performance, seems much more valid, yet often the sheer extent of Native American religious events leaves us wallowing in unfamiliar muds of data with little idea about what to do with them. Our tested methods aimed at interpreting language texts yield little. The tendency might be to follow the model of the social sciences or the historical and critical studies of the arts. But such analyses tend to atomize the events and raise narrow technical issues encouraging us to lose sight of the major concerns which initially motivate our interests.

An approach of this sort is typified by a recent study of the designs embroidered on the Hopi kachina sash. Hopis were asked to identify and indicate the significance of the various embroidered designs. After a number of interviews there seemed to be emerging a clear correlation of the responses with the interviewee's society and village affiliation. The researchers were delighted with their findings, until one Hopi man asked them why they were not interested in what was to him most important. Eagerly they inquired further, and he told them that they had not asked about the sash itself, and went on to point out that without the sash the designs could not even exist, and certainly they could not be danced by the kachinas.

We may see in this study something of a metaphor for the approach that has characterized the academic study of religion.

Students of religion have been so interested in the designs that they have not seen the sash, or to render the metaphor, generally we have been so interested in texts that we have often not seen the enactment and living of religions. We have often ignored the contexts which in some important ways far overshadow the texts in forming the religious meanings and value orientations of religious peoples. Students of religion have been interested in text often at the expense of context. The interpretation and understanding of religion has been based largely on the historical and rational content of that which is written. Since writing is largely an extension of thought, students of religion have been interested in thought at the expense of action. Since writing most commonly reflects dogma, ideals, and extraordinary experiences and events, students of religion have focused their interest on competence at the expense of performance and code at the expense of behavior.[3] What I am suggesting is that because of the approach taken, the Hopi and Navajo, along with a great many religious communities throughout the world and human history, have simply been invisible to the academic study of religion. Our very way of looking at religion is such that these cultures have nothing that we are trained to see as religion. Even today very few students of religion acknowledge anything in Native American cultures as religion except Christianity. This may seem an exaggeration, but a review of the teaching and research in the academic study of religion confirms it.

I have had to acknowledge that the territorial division between students of religion and anthropologists has been a willing one; the student of religion is a stranger to the area, and this is so because of the very definition of religion implied by the data and interpretive methods most widely engaged within the academic study of religion.

We may feel that this is a special issue restricted to Native Americans and other exclusively oral peoples of the world, but I do not believe that. My earlier hypothesis [4] that modes of communication distinguish cultures is in some important respects misleading, for all religious peoples, whether or not their languages are written, enact and live their religions; and I suspect that their lives are more informed by these actions, behaviors, objectives, and contexts than by the formal texts to which we devote so much of our attention.

I do not wish to be misunderstood. I believe that there is great value in the study of the history and meaning of sacred texts, in the study of the history of institutions, and in the study of thought; but I also believe that one of the greatest challenges facing the study of religion is to learn how to consider more fully the elements of performance, action, and behavior. This will amount to far more than an adjustment in our methods, although that will be necessary. It will amount to a radical rethinking of what we understand religion to be.

But asking fundamental questions, rethinking basic assumptions, challenging the adequacy of working definitions are not easy tasks. We are motivated to these tasks only when we have experiences that show the inadequacy of our currently held views and ways. My experiences of Native American religions have almost always convincingly revealed some inadequacy in my ability to understand. In turn I have had to rethink basic positions. This has suggested to me that the study of Native American religions can and should serve as an important catalyst in the development of the academic study of religion and culture. As we strive to know these religious traditions more fully and accurately, and as we succeed in doing so, we will be challenged to develop our knowledge of religion as a dimension of being human and our skills in the study of religion wherever it occurs.

This process by which knowledge is expanded as the result of experiencing inadequacy has been formally described by the American philosopher Charles Sanders Peirce. Peirce saw that all knowledge is gained in just this manner. He called this process of constructing hypotheses "abductive inference" or simply "abduction." Peirce's notion of abduction is highly useful in showing the importance that Native American religions can have in the academic study of religion and culture. Understanding the abductive process also provides us with the perspective from which to comprehend more fully some of the religious processes used by Native Americans.

Philosophical perspectives commonly perceive hypotheses as arising from insight or imagination; hypotheses arise in a flash of insight that is not subject to direction, criticism, or even description. Peirce did not differ in understanding hypotheses as arising from insight or in a flash, but he held that the process of creating hypotheses is subject to criticism, to description, and is therefore logical. He discussed this process he called abduction time and again throughout his life.[5]

What continued to fascinate Peirce was the frequency with which hypotheses turn out to be upheld when tested. He argued that hypotheses could not simply be random formulations, for the possible number of false and meaningless hypotheses is overwhelmingly greater than the number of true and meaningful hypotheses. Peirce wrote that were not hypotheses "much more often true than they would be by mere chance, the human race would long ago have been extirpated for its utter incapacity in the struggle for existence."[6] Peirce argued that the process of creating hypotheses must therefore be logical and describable.

In describing abduction Peirce held that a man

upon finding himself confronted with a phenomenon unlike what he would have expected under the circumstances, he looks over its features and notices some remarkable character or relation among them which he at once recognizes as being characteristic of some conception with which his mind is already stored, so that a theory is suggested which would *explain* (that is, render necessary) that which is surprising in the phenomena (2.776).[7]

Peirce described abduction in the form of the following syllogism:

The surprising fact, C, is observed;
But if A were true, C would be a matter of course;
Hence, there is reason to suspect that A is true (5.189).[8]

Hypotheses are not truths; they are guesses that arise from the imagination.[9] They need testing by logical and empirical methods, but there is a primacy and logical firstness to hypothetic inference as reflected in the following statements by Peirce:

If we are ever to learn anything or to understand phenomena at all, it must be by adbuction that this is to be brought about (5.171).

All the ideas of science come to it by the way of Abduction (5.145).

(See also 7.218 and 2.97).

Abduction was a central interest to Peirce. When his theory of abduction is stated simply, as I have done, its profundity is threatened by its seeming obviousness. Indeed, William Davis, upon reviewing Peirce's notion of abduction, suggested that

> "abduction" could be regarded as a new word for a very old philosophical insight. And this insight is that the mind has this tendency to seek out, if not impose, unity upon phenomena. The quest for unity seems to be of great intensity and seems to lie at the root of the system-building tendency in philosophy, as well as at the root of physical researches, or, really, of intellectual activity of any kind. This quest is not pernicious, but is of the essence of the life of reason.[10]

This brief description of Peirce's theory of abduction can clarify and emphasize the importance of the study of Native American religions. The academic study of religion and culture has proceeded mainly within the frame of making deductive and inductive inferences. We are all more than aware of that tired old discussion of whether or not we should be theory or data oriented; whether we should wear theories like spectacles, applying theories like templates to whatever we see, or whether we should hold these theories and methods in abeyance while we listen sensitively for the data to call forth our theories. Based upon Peirce's analysis, it may be argued that neither process of inference, induction or deduction, adds one whit of newness to our knowledge. Only through a third, though logically first, process of inference, abduction, can newness be introduced.

Supposing that newness, new theories, new principles, new explorations, is desirable, though sometimes painful, it follows that abductive inference should be clearly understood and consciously sought after and practiced, but not to the exclusion of induction and deduction. The unfortunate common distinction between the scientific and the unscientific, corresponding broadly with the practice of logical methods of inference (induction and deduction) over against the nonlogical processes described (often with an emotive edge) as "creative," "inspirational," and "imaginative" (aligning with abduction), reveals in other terms the error of much of current articulated choices in academic processes. Peirce's wisdom was in seeing that we must not choose between induction and abduction, between explaining by making rigorous scientific inference based on empirical evidence and explaining by the exercise of imagination and insight. He demonstrated that we must move back and forth between these modes of inference; he showed that they are interdependent; and he argued that they are all logical processes. The study of religion may gain from this.

But from whence does this creative process proceed? Recall that the logical motivating condition of abduction is the observation of "the surprising fact, C." In Norwood R. Hanson's consideration of the "pattern of discovery" in elementary particle physics, he sees that all the discoveries in physics, from Galileo's grappling with acceleration to Yukawa's wrestling with the idea of a meson, have involved "a search for conceptual order amongst puzzling data."[11] In the many formulations of the abductive process, in the generation of hypotheses, in the opening to newness, we find that the motivating and initiating condition is characterized by such terms as *surprising* and *puzzling*. This is logically simple and more or less obvious; if there is no disunity, no mismeaning, experienced, there is no need for explanation.

While Peirce held that abduction is describable in logical terms, he did not limit abduction to a strictly logical condition. This is revealed in his choice of the term *surprising*, which has a kinship to the terms *puzzling* used by Hanson and *incongruity* investigated so powerfully and creatively by Jonathan Z. Smith.[12] The word *surprising* focuses upon the powerful emotive or feeling dimension that Peirce understood as essential to abduction. The word refers to human emotions rather than to the logical conditions of facts. *Surprise* means to strike with a sudden feeling of unexpected wonder. The term has as much to do with the nature and tempo of the experience as with the logical nature of what is experienced. *Surprise* is synonymous with *astonishment, amazement,* and *astounding*.

Peirce understood not only that the motivating condition for abduction is based in feeling, but that the whole process engages and, in some respects, depends upon feeling. He described this aspect of abduction in elegant terms:

> Hypothesis substitutes, for a complicated tangle of predicates attached to one subject, a single conception. Now, there is

a peculiar sensation belonging to the act of thinking that each of these predicates inheres in the subject. In hypothetic [abductive] inference this complicated feeling so produced is replaced by a single feeling of greater intensity, that belonging to the act of thinking the hypothetic conclusion. Now, when our nervous system is excited in a complicated way, there being a relation between the elements of the excitation, the result is a single harmonious disturbance which I call an emotion. Thus, the various sounds made by the instruments of an orchestra strike upon the ear, and the result is a peculiar musical emotion, quite distinct from the sounds themselves. This emotion is essentially the same thing as in hypothetic inference, and every hypothetic inference involves the formation of such an emotion. We may say, therefore, that hypothesis produces the *sensuous* element of thought, and induction the *habitual* element (2.643).

Abduction then is not only motivated by a feeling, it is carried to its conclusion by a feeling; that is, hypotheses are generated in processes motivated, accompanied, and measured by feelings, emotions. Abduction or hypothetic inference produces the sensuous element of thought and is thereby a feeling kind of knowing. While it is not wholly adequate in and of itself in the production of truth, abduction is nonetheless essential to the significant advacement of knowledge and truth.

In our attempt to seek the abductive situation and to practice hypothetic inference in the academic study of religion, we must recognize that much hinges upon our being open to the experience of surprise, for the emotion of surprise is the fuel that drives the engine that generates hypotheses. Without this human experience that stimulates the sensuous element of thought, we do not create hypotheses; we do not add to our knowledge. Surprise, like disenchantment and disorientation, encourages one to change where one stands.

Peirce did not discuss this element of surprise, nor is it discussed in writings on Peirce's thought.[13] While the emotion of surprise is logically necessary, I think that there commonly exists an inordinate insensitivity to the creative powers it engenders and we practice a variety of techniques designed to short-circuit the abductive process. We desensitize ourselves to the emotion of surprise in many ways. In a logical sense these are stock hypotheses we use to terminate immediately the abductive process. There are several common types among these hypotheses. They may be articulated in the following familiar statements: 1) "I'm surprised by something, but that must be due to my ignorance." This statement implies that we willingly accept our ignorance, at least in some areas. 2) "I'm surprised by something, but I can't pay attention to every quirk; this is someone else's department." This statement reflects an atomized world of specialization where we ignore all but what is in our own purview. 3) "I'm surprised by something; 'How surprising!'" This statement acknowledges that the world does not always make sense, and to simply acknowledge surprise dispenses with the motivation to generate explanation. 4) "I'm surprised by something; indeed so surprised am I that I cannot think at all." This statement accounts for the emotion of surprise or amazement that is so great that it trips our overload switches; something like upon observing the existence of the Andromeda galaxy millions of light years away, all we can say is "Gee whiz!"

All of these stock hypotheses are frequently used, and they are indispensable. Without them we would spend our lives on the spots of our births immobilized by the inability to stop hypothesizing. Still, we must be aware that we often terminate the creative process by invoking these hypotheses out of laziness and habit.

More serious is the stance that rejects the element of surprise all together. This approach, either naïve or cosmopolitan, is reflected in statements like, "No fact, A to Z, in any context can surprise me." There are positive and negative aspects of this stance. Certainly the control over the abductive process accompanies an embracing of a confident sense of the world and occurs as one gains personal and cultural identity and maturity. Things are far less surprising when we gain knowledge of them. But this kind of stemming of the abductive process itself can also be negative if it leads to a narrow- or literal-mindedness, and most especially in academia. This most insidious deterrent to abduction rests upon an ignorance of the process of abduction itself, upon an ignorance of the generative powers of the emotion of surprise. It may take the form of a dogmatism to inductive and deductive modes of thought or to established theories. Whatever the base, the emotion of surprise is suppressed or dismissed as nonconformity, lunacy, or heresy, and it is suppressed to willfully avoid the consequences of the abductive process.

What I have wanted to suggest by focusing here on certain aspects of my experiences with Navajo and Hopi religion and culture is that, particularly in the light of Peirce's theory of abduction, exposure to Native American religions and cultures presents us with a high degree of probability that we will feel surprise, astonishment, and amazement in what we experience, and that these feelings will instigate, if we allow them, the abductive process.

In the essays that follow I want to demonstrate the fruitfulness of this approach which I call religion by abduction. I want to show not only the wonderful richness of many aspects of Native American religions, but to take advantage of the coincident abductive process that stimulates the further inquiry into the nature of religion as a dimension of being human and as a field of academic inquiry.

NOTES

1. See, e.g., Dell Hymes, "The Americanist Tradition," in *American Indian Languages and American Linguistics*, ed. Wallace L. Chafe (Lisse: The Peter de Ridder Press, 1976), pp. 11-28.
2. Among these scholars are Åke Hultkrantz, Joseph Epes Brown, Karl Luckert, Howard Harrod and Christopher Vecsey.
3. This is true also in the study of language, as articulated in a lecture, much influential to my thinking, by Michael Silverstein, "Metaforces of Power in Traditional Oratory," delivered at Yale and the University of Chicago, Spring, 1981.
4. This hypothesis is explored in my book *Beyond "the Primitive": The Religions of Nonliterate Peoples* (Englewood Cliffs, NJ: Prentice-Hall, 1982).
5. K. T. Fann's study, *Peirce's Theory of Abduction* (The Hague: Martinus Nijhoff, 1970), clarifies Peirce's writings on abduction by showing that it was a regular concern throughout his intellectual life, appearing very early in his writing, and changing significantly with the development of his thought. The theory gained its fullest coherence in Peirce's writings after 1900, and if the history of the development of Peirce's thought on abduction is not accounted for, considerable confusion may result. My concern here is not so much with Peirce's development of the theory

but rather with the theory itself as finally developed and with the many implications it has for our studies.

6. Charles S. Peirce, Ms. 692, as quoted in Thomas A. Sebeok, "One, Two, Three Spells U B E R T Y (in lieu of an introduction)," in *The Sign of Three: Dupin, Holmes, Peirce*, ed. Umberto Eco and Thomas A. Sebeok (Bloomington: Indiana University Press, 1983), p. 17.

7. References to Peirce's works will be given by volume and paragraph numbers from Charles Sanders Peirce, *Collected Papers*, vols. 1–6 ed. C. Hartshorne and P. Weiss; vols. 7–8 ed. A. W. Burks, (Cambridge: Harvard University Press, 1931–1958).

8. Peirce was concerned with how abduction differs from induction. He changed his mind on the matter many times. For a discussion of this distinction see 2.624.

9. Peirce utilized the term *guess* frequently to characterize hypothesis and theory. For discussions of the term see Charles Sanders Peirce, "Guessing," *The Hound and the Horn* 2 (1929): 267-82 and *Collected Papers* 5.181 and 8.385.

10. William H. Davis, "Synthetic Knowledge as 'Abduction,'" *Southern Journal of Philosophy*, Spring 1970, 40.

11. Norwood R. Hanson, *Patterns of Discovery: An Inquiry into the Conceptual Foundations of Science* (Cambridge: Cambridge University Press, 1965), p. 119.

12. "A Pearl of Great Price and a Cargo of Yams: A Study in Situational Incongruity," in Jonathan Z. Smith, *Imagining Religion: From Babylon to Jonestown* (Chicago: The University of Chicago Press, 1982), pp. 90-101.

13. The closest is Peirce's discussion of "doubt" and "the fixation of belief" (5.370–87), which parallels in some respects my following discussion of stock hypotheses that terminate the abductive process.

The Trees Stood
Deep Rooted

Some time ago I went to hear Indian elders speak about public education programs for Indians. An old Papago man was among them. When his turn came, he rose slowly, and with deliberation began to speak. His style was formal and bore an air of certainty, though for his meaning I had to await the English interpretation. He began with the creation of the Papago world by telling how Earthmaker had given the Papago land its shape and character. He identified the features of that creation with the land on which he had always lived, as had his father and all his grandfathers before him. Pausing in his story, he asked how many of us could locate our heritage so distinctly. Then he went on to tell the stories of Iitoi who had acted as protector and teacher of the Papago under the name Elder Brother. He told of the way of life of the Papago people, a way of life they have always enjoyed.

It was perhaps fifteen minutes before he began to speak directly to the subject of education, but the old man had been talking about education all along. He was demonstrating to his audience a basic principle in education: knowledge has meaning and value only when placed within a particular view of the world. He was utilizing the way of his people by consulting the stories of the creation for the proper perspective from which to speak. There was power in his words and his statement was convincing.

As a Papago elder this old man understood the power of relating the stories of creation. Papago culture abounds in songs and poems ritually uttered in order to provide sustenance and to maintain the Papago way of life. They are the gifts of the gods, not the works of man. Some are attributed to Iitoi, who used them to win battles against enemies. The Papago identify the ruins which are found throughout their southern Arizona desert homelands as the villages of these enemy peoples. The Papago people have songs and poems which they recognize as capable of affecting nearly every aspect of life. The feeling of the power the people find in these words is captured in the beautiful lines of one of their poems.

> With my songs the evening spread echoing
> And the early dawn emerged with a good sound.
> The firm mountains stood echoing therewith
> And the trees stood deep rooted.[1]

The Papago are not unique among Native Americans in recognizing a kind of performative power in the language of their songs, prayers, and poems. In his eloquent address "The Man Made of Words," N. Scott Momaday said, "Whenever the Indian ponders over the mystery of origin he shows a tendency to ascribe to the word a creative power all its own. The word is conceived of as an independent entity, superior even to the gods." According to Momaday, the Native American "locates the center of his being within the element of language. . . . It is the dimension in which his existence is most fully accomplished. He does not create language but is himself created within it. In a real sense, his language is both the object and the instrument of his religious experience."[2]

The repetitive nature of Native American prayer and song has caused some observers to declare them to be merely the recitation of magical formulas. This is a view to be guarded against. The magic of the word lies mainly in the fact that it is capable, through image and symbol, of placing the speaker in communication with his own being and with the whole world. Native Americans do not restrict language to its capacity to describe the world; they recognize that, from one perspective, it is the world.

There seems to be a remarkable link between the stories of origin and the lifeways of Native Americans. It seems to me that this link is the language of ritual that constitutes Native American religious traditions. The events of creation are somehow paradigmatic, and the knowledge given in the creation stories permeates the life of the people.

To the Navajo the world was not created by some powerful earth-making god, but through the creative powers of thought and the ritual language of song and prayer. Indeed, thought and speech were personified prior to the creation of the world. They arose from the medicine bundle out of which all creation was to come, and they were said to embody the powers of the bundle. They took the form of a young man and woman of such radiance and beauty that they could scarcely be looked upon. While they were to be present in this form for only a brief time, it was told that they would always be near to the world, for theirs are the powers that sustain life. Their names are often rendered in English as Long Life Boy (thought) and Happiness Girl (speech), reflecting the Navajo view that their names are synonymous with the highest measure of life.

The Navajo ceremonial Blessingway demonstrates how the Navajo envision the way thought and speech became manifest in the creation of the world and in the sustenance of life. Of the twenty-five or thirty major ceremonial ways known to the Navajo, Blessingway is generally recognized as fundamental to all others; it is an indivisible body of story and ritual and a whole religious ideology. The Navajo name for Blessingway, *hózhǫ́ǫ́jí*, reflects the pervasive ideology of creation that supports this ceremonial; a literal translation would be something like "the way to secure an environment of perfect beauty." The occasion for the first performance of a Blessingway ceremonial was the creation of the Navajo world; consequently the way of creation is the model for all versions and all performances of Blessingway. It is because Blessingway is the way of creation that it is called the backbone of Navajo religion and is recognized as the source and pattern of the Navajo way of life and thought.

In Blessingway stories the first act in the creation of the world was the building of a ceremonial structure in which the ritual acts of creation could be performed. A version of Blessingway, therefore, is performed on the occasion of the construction of a Navajo house. But Blessingway is also incorporated into all other ceremonials as the first-performed rite in order to "bless" the structure in which the rituals are to be carried out—whether the occasion be marriage, the need for rain, or difficult or imminent childbirth. In the story prototype the humanlike beings who were performing the ritual began to construct the ceremonial house. Significantly, these humanlike beings who preceded the creation of the world are known by the Navajo word *yałti'ii*, which means "speaker." They readied the support poles and leaned them into position. As the support poles were readied and dropped into place, songs named them and described their placement and significance.

> Along below the east, Earth's pole I
>   first lean into position
> As I plan for it it drops,
> As I speak to it it drops,
> Now it listens to me as it drops,
> It yields to my wish as it drops.
> Long life drops, happiness drops into
>   position *ni yo o.*[3]

And below the south, Mountain Woman's pole is leaned into position, followed by Water Woman's pole below the west and Corn Woman's pole below the north.

The house described in this ceremony provides the pattern for the common Navajo conical-style hogan. It serves the Navajo both as a place of residence and as a ceremonial structure. But the song identifies the four main poles of this simple substructure with the pillars that support the Navajo world. The foundations of the poles are located below the horizon in the four cardinal directions. Each pillar is named and given the power to sustain life through its identification with long life (thought) and happiness (speech). The commonplace Navajo home is at the same time the structure of the entire Navajo world.

This linkage between the most commonplace and the most ethereal, made through ritual language, is illustrated even more powerfully in the imagery, found in a Navajo Nightway prayer, of the house whose structure is composed of the life forms of the earth:

> House made of dawn,
> House made of evening twilight,
> House made of dark cloud,
> House made of male rain,
> House made of dark mist,
> House made of female rain,
> House made of pollen,
> House made of grasshoppers.[4]

Each phrase focuses the mind on an image of the finite, material, domestic dwelling only to explore that image into fantastic dimensions by identifying its composition with unexpected building materials. A unity is achieved through the lines in their creation of an image of a living universe.

Navajo sand painting also illustrates the way in which creation is fundamental in Navajo life. Paintings made of crushed vegetal materials or ground minerals and rocks are ritually constructed and used as part of several Navajo ceremonials. Hundreds of them have been recorded, and their designs and meanings are remarkably complex. Without accounting for all the occasions in which sand paintings are used, the ritual acts performed upon them, or the various scholarly interpretations made of them, it can be shown that the efficacy of the sand-painting act is derived from the events in the creation of the Navajo world.

In the Blessingway story it is told that after the "speakers" built the creation hogan, they entered it and proceeded with the creation. From the medicine bundle they took pieces of white shell, abalone, turquoise, and jet. With these materials they constructed representations on the floor of all forms of life that were to be in the Navajo world. These forms of life were personified as holy people having humanlike forms. The ritual construction was like a sand painting. Each holy being represented was given identity by its dress and placement relative to the others. The resulting design was not a physical model of Navajo land, but rather a map of the Navajo religious conception of the world.

The creation concluded with the intoning of a long prayer to these holy people, who represented the life forms of the earth. The prayer associated and identified them with the physical universe and consequently effected an indivisible unity between the ritual world of the ceremonial hogan of creation and the ordinary world of the Navajo, a unity of the spiritual and the material. A world had been made using only simple materials and the creative powers of thought and speech. Based on this model, Navajos continue to perform acts of creation through the power of representation in sand paintings and the ritual language of song and prayer.

Following the creation the life forms known as Dawn and Evening Twilight went on a tour to inspect the new world. Upon ascending mountaintops to gain a vantage point, they found the scene around them to be extremely beautiful. This state of pristine creation is articulated by the Navajo people in many ways, and it stands as the inspiration and measure of Navajo life. Life is envisioned as a journey down a road. It is deemed a good life if the traveler is surrounded by an environment of beauty comparable to that of the newly created world. Most Navajo prayers conclude with a passage describing this good life:

> With beauty before me may I walk
> With beauty behind me may I walk
> With beauty above me may I walk
> With beauty below me may I walk
> With beauty all around me may I walk
> As one who is long life and happiness may I walk
>
> In beauty it is finished.
> In beauty it is finished.

Through the utterance of the prayer one is placed once again on the good road, so that it may be said with confidence and feeling, "In beauty it is finished."

There is yet another way to show how the events of creation are paradigmatic for Navajo lifeways. This centers on the importance in Navajo culture of the possession of a mountain-soil bundle. After the world was created, but before it was made suitable for habitation by Navajo people, a girl child was created. Her parents are said to be the beautiful youth and maiden, Long Life Boy and Happiness Girl. This child had the remarkable ability to grow older through time, to reach old age, and to repeat the cycle of life again and again. Because of this she was called Changing Woman. Changing Woman was given a medicine bundle containing objects and powers that created the world. The bundle was the source of her own existence, since her parents were the personification of the powers it held. Changing Woman was also taught the creation rituals. With the bundle and the Blessingway songs and prayers Changing Woman at once holds and represents the power of creation. She personifies the perfect beauty secured in the creation. She is identified with the newly created earth. She is the source and sustenance of all life. She is time. She is the mother of the Navajo people.

After her birth Changing Woman used her creative powers to make the earth ready and suitable for the Navajo people. She created the plants and animals and cleared the world of the monsters who had come to threaten human life. Having made the earth a suitable place, she created the Navajo people. Her final act before departing from the Navajo world was to pass the knowledge of Blessingway on to the Navajo people. In doing so, she charged them with the responsibility to maintain the world in its state of perfect beauty by the use of Blessingway. She warned them that the Blessingway songs should never be forgotten, for Navajo life depends upon them.

Changing Woman is wholly benevolent and of such beauty that she is rarely represented in any visual form in Navajo ceremonies. But she did show the Navajo how to make a bundle modeled on hers; this was the origin of the mountain-soil bundle. It is made with soil ritually collected from the four sacred mountains which stand in the quarters of the Navajo world. The soil from each mountain is wrapped in buckskin. Maintaining the directional orientations, these four bags are placed around stone representations of Long Life Boy and Happiness Girl. A buckskin is wrapped around all this and the bundle is secured.

The mountain-soil bundle is the nuclear ritual object in Blessingway. Many Navajo families keep bundles as guides to the Navajo way of life and as sources of long life and happiness for the family. The bundle holds the powers of creation. It is the source of life and the paragon of perfect beauty established by Blessingway.

Navajo people often refer to the relationship of their many ceremonial ways as the branches of a tree which extend over every occasion, bearing and protecting the Navajo way of life. They identify Blessingway as the trunk of this tree which supports all other ceremonial branches. This tree stands deep rooted in the creation of the world.

Certainly the Navajo are not representative of all Native American peoples, nor should they be considered typical. Even in the American Southwest the Navajo are only one among many cultures that contain a wide variety of lifeways and religious practices. While there is tremendous diversity within Native American cultures, certain general observations may be drawn from the Navajo example.

We have seen that the Navajo find in the story of their origin a paradigm for their lifeways and religious practices. The story of origin serves at once as a prototype for a ceremonial performance and as a wellspring of philosophy and world view. A distinctive characteristic of this paradigm is the way in which it unifies the primordial and physical geographies, the ethereal and the common-place, and the spiritual and the material. Frequently the best-known passages from Native American literature are ones that illustrate this correlation. Often these passages describe an association of four to seven directions or world categories with colors, animals, birds, eras, and certain qualities or temperaments.

To many such well-defined patterns have suggested that Native Americans live in simple harmonious integration with the world around them. But in light of the Navajo views of creation we should reexamine this common assumption that Native Americans are sim-ple children of nature, for I believe we will find it erroneous. Native Americans have shown themselves to be masters of survival in an environment that has often been reluctant to nurture them, but their lifeways can scarcely be called the simple following of natural instincts. It seems almost the opposite. The Navajo, for example, look upon no living thing as simply natural, as a product of some impersonal system of natural law. Life is dependent upon holy people who were created in the beginning and who stand within all living things. Many Native Americans can hold a person-to-person relationship with their environment or some aspects of it because in their view of creation, the power of life, which has personhood, is united with and identical to the physical living world. The nature of these personal relationships is not determined by the aspirations of ego as much as by patterns established in the stories, songs, and prayers.

There is also a tendency to assume that the paradigms which arise from the stories of creation represent Native Americans views of the permanent status of their world. But these patterns of perfect beauty serve more as an objective and a measure in life than as a description of it. Underlying these global representations of the ideal are infinitely complex principles of relationship which deter-mine and direct the lifeways. In the whole range of human action nothing is exempt. In other words, for many Native Americans all human action is continually measured against traditional patterns so that the way life is experienced is dependent upon how it is lived.

Through a tradition of formal ritual acts Native Americans can relate to the world, find the significance of life, and uphold the responsibility for maintaining order as it was given to the world in the beginning. In this view their ritual acts are creative acts of the highest order, since the object of their creation is the world itself. The greatest human responsibility is to perform the acts upon which life and reality depend.

The Native American view of human creativity is based in religion, not in art. Such a stance is not void of excitement and illumination, for it is the creative genius of the Native American way of life to see the uncommon in the common, to find the ethereal in the mundane. Theirs is the way longed for by Artur Sammler, the protagonist in Saul Bellow's novel *Mr. Sammler's Planet*, who said, "And what is 'common' about 'the common life'? What if some genius were to do with 'common life' what Einstein did with 'matter'? Finding its energetics, uncovering its radiance."[5] When deep rooted in creation, Native American traditions energize the common life.

NOTES

1. Ruth Underhill, *Singing for Power: The Song Magic of the Papago Indians of Southern Arizona* (Berkeley and Los Angeles: University of California Press, 1968).
2. N. Scott Momaday, "The Man Made of Words," *Indian Voices: The First Convocation of American Indian Scholars* (San Francisco: Indian Historian Press, 1970), pp. 49-62.
3. Leland C. Wyman, *Blessingway* (Tucson: University of Arizona Press, 1970), p. 115.
4. Washington Matthews, *Night Chant, a Navajo Ceremony* (New York: American Museum of Natural History Memoirs, vol. 6, 1902), p. 143.
5. Saul Bellow, *Mr. Sammler's Planet* (New York: Viking Press, 1969), p. 147.

The Shadow of a Vision Yonder

While my family and I were living with a Navajo family north of Tuba City, Arizona, I witnessed an ordinary social event that at the time I thought to be curious but of little consequence. Since then I have found occasion to reflect upon that event. From it I think I learned something about the Navajo way of life, even something about their religion, which is the subject I had gone there to pursue. I confess that I went to the Navajo reservation not very well prepared to do fieldwork. I had not done enough homework to afford me the clearest view of my contact with Navajo people. As a result, much of what I was to learn came to me through insightful flashbacks some time after I had left Navajo country.

By midsummer we had become well enough acquainted with our Navajo family to be trusted with some of their work. I considered it an honor to be asked to help hoe the weeds in the cornfield they had planted in the valley below the beautiful mesa on which we lived. Being from a farming family in Kansas, I willingly accepted the invitation and replied that I would gladly hoe the corn. To my dismay our Navajo friends expressed alarm. I am sure they were considering how they could retract the invitation as they told me, "Oh no, we don't hoe the *corn*, we hoe the weeds!" I assured them that I really did know the difference between corn plants and the unwanted weeds and that it was just the way we described the job back home. It was simply a product of the peculiarity of my own language, not theirs.

After getting the younger children on their way with the sheep, we headed for the cornfield early the next morning. Under cautious eyes I set about proving that I not only knew the difference between weeds and corn; but that I was no slouch with a hoe. Of course I was never to know the extent of my success. The weight of my experience with the Navajo people is that their quiet dignity always prevails.

With my flashing hoe gradually slowing to match the ordered, rhythmic movement of the other hoes—the native hoes—I was relieved when late in the morning it was time to stop for lunch. Moving to the arbor or "shade," a small, partly enclosed brush structure, we took lunch. Then we prepared to rest for several hours during the heat of the day. It was in the shade that I was to observe the event on which I want to reflect.

The shade was perhaps half mile from a narrow dirt road. In that part of the country the traffic is not what one would call heavy. During the quiet rest period after lunch I was aroused from my drowsiness a couple of times by a soft but excited discussion of whatever motor vehicle, usually a pickup truck, passed by on the road. I noticed that all present expressed interest in the traffic. They arose and peered through the open areas in the brush on the side of the shade facing the road. I recalled the many times I had driven up to a Navajo dwelling, finding absolutely no sign of human activity.

What surprised me was the response my friends made when one of the passing pickups turned off the road and headed toward our shade. Watching with rapt attention, my Navajo friends carefully timed it so that as the truck pulled up to the shade and stopped, every member of the family was actively occupied. The grandmother sat on the ground with her back to the entrance near the truck and began her spinning. The children played a game in the dirt of the shade floor. Others sat about, gazing across the landscape, always in a direction away from the truck. This directed all attention away from the presence of the visitors.

The visitors in the truck were Navajos and knew how to respond. They sat in the truck for some minutes. It seemed like a very long time to me. Then quietly the man, his wife, and young daughter left their truck to enter the edge of the shade. There they sat upon the ground. The man quietly restrained the eagerness of the little girl to play with the other children. Again some minutes passed while my family continued their spinning, playing, and gazing. Finally the man spoke a few soft words to the grandmother, who gently, almost inaudibly, responded without turning her head toward him. In a few minutes he spoke again. This quiet conversation continued for some time; then the visitors arose and moved about the shade, talking softly to each of us, including me, extending their hands for a handshake and speaking the Navajo greeting, *yá'át'ééh*. Next my friends arose and began to intermingle with the visitors. I was informed that they were going to the trading post some ten miles away to get water and supplies to prepare a meal for the visitors. The entire proceedings had taken more than a quarter of an hour.

The insight that has come to me through continued reflection is that the incident illustrates the "way" of Navajo religion. I had witnessed the performance of a formal ritual for purposes of establishing certain kinds of social relationships, in this instance between Navajo families. The ritual reflects the quiet dignity and the patient and formal manner of the Navajo people. And by its simplicity it helps place the almost infinite complexity of Navajo ceremonies in a better perspective. It also gives clues regarding the nature of Navajo religion, wherein relationships are established or reestablished with the holy ones.

Notice that the situation had been carefully analyzed by my Navajo friends. They followed proper conduct with deliberateness and patience. This resulted in the successful establishing of a relationship between two families. Each party made some sign to show that it understood its obligations and was committing itself to their fulfillment. The guests offered their hands as a sign of their entrance into the relationship. My family proceeded to meet their first obligation of the relationship by offering a meal to the guests.

It is commonly observed that Navajo religion centers largely on the rituals by which an individual who is suffering a malady is healed. The sufferer is attended to by an individual called a "singer." The singer directs the ritual activities and is responsible for knowing the songs, prayers, and the order of the ritual processes. A Navajo ceremony is not performed unless it is called for. But when it is called for, the family of the sufferer must arrange with a singer to perform the ceremony. This requires making a formal relationship through social and ritual acts not unlike those characteristic of the introduction to which I have made reference. In both settings the relationship is bonded through a formal sign. In this case the singer receives payment in material goods or cash in return for performing the ceremony. David Aberle has analyzed this exchange and has convincingly shown that the "fee" is not really payment for services rendered, but is a sign of the establishment of a reciprocity relationship.[1] The singer is thus obliged to respond by conducting the requested ceremonial.

In the performance of Navajo ceremonies the observer is struck by the material insignificance of the ritual objects. He also cannot help but notice the extreme care and formality with which these objects are treated. A singer's medicine bundle consists of nothing more precious than an odd assortment of sticks, feathers, bags of colored sands and vegetal materials, rocks, and so on. These things appear so common, even crude, that it makes one wonder how they could have any religious significance. But in the context of ritual the same objects are carefully handled, described in song, explicated in prayer, and manipulated in ritual. Their significance is developed to such a magnitude that they infinitely surpass their material content.

This is in keeping with the Navajo story of creation. The story utilizes common objects in describing the process of bringing life to the world. First Man, who directed the creation, had a medicine bundle containing bits of colored rocks called "jewels." First Man carefully placed these "jewels" upon the floor of the creation hogan to designate the life forces of the things that were to be created. All life forms were represented in these mundane substances, and their distinguishing characteristics were understood to be exemplified in the shapes of the jewels. Furthermore, the relative place where each was laid on the floor of the creation hogan designated the place each was to occupy in the world, together with the relationship each was to have to all other living things. These material representations of life were then clothed in a layer of colored sands to represent the outward appearance they would have in the created world. After the preparation of this microcosm had been completed, prayers were uttered to transform the ritual creation into the more visible everyday world of the Navajos. This is the way in which the Navajos conceive the process of the creation of their world. When creation was completed, the world was beautiful. All things were formed and set in a place, and proper relationships existed among them.

In both the creation of the world and the creation of the social relationships formalities dominate. The formal enactment of ritual brings things to their proper place and serves to interconnect them by establishing binding relationships. Ritual acts are understood to be essential to the establishing of proper relationships. Navajo life depends upon such relationships.

Scholarly interpretation does not always catch the significance of this. Frequently the interpretation of Navajo religion has called attention to the performance of "magical" acts. They are called magical to indicate that there is no ordinary causal principle that connects the acts performed with the expected results. I would never want to dismiss the presence of mystery and magic in Navajo religion. Yet it seems to me that the more significant factor is the process by which the visions and great conceptions are communicated by the formal manipulation of mundane objects. Let me illustrate the difference. The most common scholarly interpretation of the sand-painting rite is that it contains a kind of magical osmosis. The sand painting is prepared upon the floor of the ceremonial hogan, the sufferer enters and sits upon the sand painting, and the singer applies sands from the figures represented in the painting to the person. At the conclusion of the rite the sand paintings are formally destroyed and removed from the ceremonial hogan. According to the magical osmosis explanation the sand painting is understood to absorb the illness or the evil cause of the illness, taking it from the one suffering and replacing it with goodness from the sand painting. This explanation focuses attention on the removal of the sands after the rite, for it resembles and builds upon similarities between this act and the removal of sands into which one vomits in emetic rites.

In my view this magical osmosis interpretation is partially if not wholly in error. I would propose instead that sand-painting rites are meaningful curing acts because of the Navajos' recognition of the performative powers of ritual representation. In preparing the sand painting the Navajos follow the precedent established in the processes of world creation. In Navajo creation stories it is said that in the beginning the forces of life were set forth in material form by arranging common objects of several colors upon the floor of a ceremonial hogan. Thus, in physical representations using ordinary materials Navajos express their conception of the profound nature of life. In a healing ceremony the sand paintings are closely associated with the elements identified with the cause of the illness suffered. As is told in the story of each ceremonial, the sand paintings are revealed to the hero as he or she is being cured of an illness. In most cases the illness is due to the fact that something is out of its proper place—for example, a ghost who will not remain in its domain, a person who has made contact with the dead, a deity who has been angered or offended by a person who has trespassed or violated a taboo, or a witch who has gained power by being out of bounds. The causal agent rather than the illness suffered determines the nature of the ceremonial cure. The ritual presents the forces of life in the shape and relative places assigned to them as recounted in the stories. The identification of the person treated with the sand painting by touching the sands of the parts of the body of the painted figures to the corresponding parts of his or her body is a gesture of communicating proper relationships. This is very similar to the acts performed to place the forces of life represented on the floor of the creation hogan within the representations of the outward forms they were to take in the world. And, as in the case of the process of world creation, the formal removal of the sand paintings designates a transition from the world of ritual to the world thus represented.

Relationships are central to the Navajo way of life. Life's interrelationships are not casual. They are the product of careful ritual prescription, which acts to both bind and reestablish a proper order of relationships. In the Navajo conception life and good health are not so much a matter of substance as they are a matter of form and place with respect to the rest of the created world. Each living thing has an identity, a proper place, and a way to be. This identity, place, and way must be honored and carefully maintained.

The Navajo way of life can be characterized at one level as a kind of formalism, although Navajos would not describe it in this way. The Navajos' own appreciation of ritual form becomes particularly compelling in their belief about the curative power of the healing rites. Here the objects and acts presented are appreciated for having the power to cure physical illness, and the Navajo have in mind something quite different from our common reduction of their religion to a kind of primitive psychology. In the enactment of their religion they recognize a power to change the shape of things in the world, even when the materials they engage in these enactments are mundane. Such acts make earthly elements into a vehicle disclosing the deepest forces of life.

The performance of a sand-painting rite is in a way comparable to the shaking of hands to seal a social relationship. Both of these acts reflect the same temperament. Both indicate the way in which Navajos apprehend reality. In both cases mundane ingredients reveal deeper significance. There is nothing special in the handshake, for example. But in the context of the formal ritual of establishing relationships, handshaking performs an essential role by assuring each party of the acceptance of the privileges and obligations of the relationship. It marks transformation from a relationship discussed to a relationship established and made operative. Similarly, in Navajo sand painting rites the substance of the colored sands is not as important as the shapes which they form. Properly prepared and used, the sand painting has the power to cure. It reestablishes for the sufferer the proper relationships with the forces of life on which his or her health and happiness depend. In this regard one of the most important components of Native American religions is the process by which concepts of being and becoming are represented and communicated through the use of acts and objects. I have cited one instance of this in Navajo religion. The same phenomenon occurs in Hopi culture.

I remember feeling confused when I first learned that Hopi children witness an event which they find shocking and bitterly disappointing at the conclusion of their first religious initiation. I am referring to the conclusion of the initiation into the kachina cult, which is composed of two societies, the Kachina Society and the Powamu Society. Formally this initiation begins the religious life of all Hopi children, boys and girls alike. The event occurs as a part of the Bean Dance, which concludes the annual celebration of Powamu, a late winter ceremonial to prepare for the agricultural cycle. The newly initiated children are escorted into a kiva, an underground ceremonial chamber, there to await the entrance of the kachinas, the masked dancers they have come to know as Hopi spirit messengers. Prior to this time the already initiated go to great efforts to keep the children from discovering that kachinas are masked male members of their own village. Announcing that they are kachinas, the dancers enter the kiva where the children are eagerly awaiting them. But they appear for the first time to the new initiates without their masks. The children immediately recognize the identity of the dancing figures. Their response is shock, disappointment, and bitterness.

It would seem to me that this concluding event in the Powamu ceremonial leaves the children in a peculiarly unstable state as new initiates. I would have expected the purpose of the initiaton to be to reveal clearly the full nature of the kachinas to the children. But it appears that the initiation rites accomplish only the destruction of the belief in the identity of the kachina figures held by the children prior to the initiation. Margaret Mead likened this event to the European-American child learning of the identity of Santa Claus, which is often accompanied by the same kind of bitter disappointment. There are surface similarities, but this is not a satisfactory explanation. Nor should we accept another common scholarly interpretation: that it is inevitable the children learn that kachinas are not real gods, but men dressed as gods. We may find some force in this argument, since, as outside occasional observers, we can easily recognize that the kachina dancers are masked mortals. Even when a Hopi says that in donning the kachina mask he "becomes the kachina," we tend to offer a critical interpretation. A play theory has also been advanced. This position argues that the Hopi acts "as if" he were a kachina and makes the statement while he is so pretending. But all of these interpretations are found wanting.

Instead, it is important that we take seriously what the initiated Hopi says. We must recognize that he actually means what he says, that in putting on the kachina mask he really becomes a kachina. This is a clear statement on his part. It is in light of this statement that we should attempt to see how at the conclusion of the initiation the shadow cast on the kachina figures serves to reveal to the children the true nature of the kachinas. The ceremony appears to be deliberately calculated to engender the disappointment the children feel.

A fuller review of the contextual events is necessary.[2] Prior to the initiation into the kachina cult the children, largely under the age of ten, are carefully guided into the development of a particular kind of relationship with the kachinas. The kachinas, who frequent the villages during only half of the year, have a wide range of contacts with the children. Many of them are kind and benevolent to the children, presenting them with gifts. Others are frightening ogres who discipline naughty children by threatening to eat them. And some are silly clowns who entertain the children with their antics. In all of these contacts the uninitiated children are protected against seeing kachinas unmasked or the masks unoccupied. They are also guarded against hearing anything that might disclose the masked character of the kachina figures. The children are told that the kachinas come to the village from their spirit homes far away to overlook and direct the affairs of the Hopi people. They are taught that they too will become kachinas when they die. Prior to the initiation events the children grow to accept the familiar kachina figures as being exactly what they appear to be.

The perspective nurtured in the children is given its final stage of development in the kachina cult initiation rites. During the Powamu ceremonial to which the initiation rites are attached, the initiates are given special attention by the kachinas. They come into closer contact. The kachinas give the children special gifts. They are instructed in kachina lore. All of this seems to be carefully calculated to intensify the shock the children will feel when they observe the unmasked appearance of the kachinas during the Bean Dance.

When the kachinas enter the kiva, in one sharp and sudden blow the expectations so carefully nurtured are forever shattered. For the moment only pain and bitterness take their place. But even with the disappointment life goes on, and the initiated child is given the privilege of participating in religious events. In time he or she can enter other religious societies and enjoy expanded privileges of participation. But once initiated into the kachina cult, the child can never again view religious events naïvely. Unforgettably clear to the children is the realization that some things are not what they appear to be. This realization precedes the appreciation of the full nature of reality.

This brings us back to the question of truth regarding the Hopi statement that when one dons the kachina mask he becomes a kachina. Given the appreciation by the initiated Hopi of the full nature of reality in both its material and spiritual aspects, the truth of the statement can be more clearly understood. By donning the kachina mask a Hopi gives life and action to the mask, thus making the kachina spirit present in material form. We, as uninitiated outsiders, observe only the material form. The spiritual aspect of the kachina is present as well, but that can be perceived only by the initiated. The material presence without the spiritual is mere imper-sonation—a dramatic performance, a work of art. The spiritual without the material remains unmanifest; it leaves no object for thought or speech or action. The spiritual must reside in some manifest form to be held in common by the community. The view, often taken, that the kachinas are merely impersonations fails to recognize the full religious nature of the kachina performances. It also fails to take into account the truth of the statement. If the kachinas are not present in both material and spiritual form, the events could scarcely be called religious.

Both Navajo and Hopi religions evidence an appreciation for the power of ritual performance, for in this way are the surfaces of reality penetrated. On the one hand, the mundane materials which comprise religious objects and actions must never be taken as being more than the simple ordinary earthy and human elements they are. This fact is driven home in the disenchantment with the material appearance of the kachinas experienced by the children undergoing initiation. It is also evident in the example of the sand-painting rite from Navajo culture. On the other hand, the ordinary materials when presented in the proper form manifest the spiritual, or reveal the deeper meanings of life. Both Navajo sand paintings and Hopi kachinas have the power to order and profoundly affect the world.

I think that this deep appreciation for this process of manifesta-tion and investigation is broadly held among Native Americans, as among most religious cultures. A fine illustration of this is found in the wisdom of the Oglala Sioux, Black Elk, as told to John Neihardt in *Black Elk Speaks*, although the role of Neihardt as editor is questionable. As a youth Black Elk was the recipient of a remark-able vision which he looked to as a guide throughout his life. For many years he kept the vision to himself, fearing to tell others. But as time went on, he found rising within him an even greater fear. Part of the message given him was that he was to enact the vision in ritual form for the people to see. This was a common practice among the Dakota. An old medicine man from whom Black Elk sought guidance warned him that if the vision were not performed, something very bad would happen to him.

Under Black Elk's direction preparations were immediately begun so that the vision could be enacted by the people. Black Elk recalls how he experienced the enactment of his vision: "I looked about me and could see that what we then were doing was like a shadow cast upon the earth from yonder vision in the heavens, so bright it was and clear. I knew the real was yonder and the darkened dream of it was here."[3]

There is a sense in which the Navajo sand paintings, the Hopi kachina masks, and many other Native American ritual acts share the properties of a shadow of a vision yonder. I have stressed that it is the form more than the substance that is important in manifesting the more profound forces of life. Certainly this is characteristic of shadows. There is a "thinness" to ritual objects and acts; they are meaningful only when cast in the light of the "yonder vision." This fragility is illustrated in the Navajo sand paintings, which are destroyed in the very acts by which they are of service. All of this is a constant reminder that the material vehicles exist and are meaningful only in the degree to which they lead beyond their own obvious limitations.

Were it not for these shadows cast by the vision yonder, Native American religions would be confined to the experience of rarified mystical moments or the internally borne knowledge of tradition. The shadow may appear bright and clear as it did to Black Elk, or dark and foreboding as it does to Hopi kachina cult initiates, but the shadows integrate Native American religions with distinctive ways of living and interpreting life.

NOTES

1. David F. Aberle, "The Navajo Singer's 'Fee': Payment or Prestation?" in *Studies in Southwestern Ethnolinguistics: Meaning and History in the Languages of the American Southwest*, ed. Dell H. Hymes and William E. Bittle, (The Hague: Mouton, 1967), pp. 15-32.
2. The full analysis is presented below in the chapter "Disenchantment: A Religious Abduction."
3. John Neihardt, *Black Elk Speaks* (New York: Pocket Books, 1972), p. 142.

"It's Where You Put Your Eyes"

"Attention to the world's art historians!" was the message sent forth in 1885 by the Army physician Washington Matthews upon observing that Navajos routinely destroy their own sand paintings.[1] He was deeply impressed with the beauty and elaboration of these paintings in sand, but that only heightened the shock of the feature he was calling to the attention of the world. A number of people work to make a sand painting; on the same day they willfully destroy it. Matthews declared these paintings to be the most transient works of art in the world. We know that such short-lived works are not unique to the Navajo, but I don't think that Matthews' cry has been seriously considered. Perhaps that is because it would raise grave questions about the way we see and understand the nature of Native American art. Now, over a century later, I would like to consider some of the questions that echo from Matthews' message.

A description of Navajo sand painting will give us a place to begin. It is a ritual procedure in Navajo culture which is part of certain religious ceremonials performed to cure an ailing person. The sand painting is constructed on the floor of a ceremonial hogan and depicts mythic persons who have a connection with the cause of the illness being treated. It must be carefully replicated according to the memory of the officiating singer or medicine man. No visual record is kept by the Navajo people, but hundreds of different patterns are known to exist. The finished picture, like a costume and mask, provides a physical form in which the spiritual beings may manifest their presence. When cornmeal is sprinkled by the singer on the painting and the person for whom the ceremony is being performed, the holy people are present in the sand painting. The rite identifies the ailing person, who walks onto and sits in the middle of

37

the painting, with each of the holy people present in it. The identification is physically accomplished by a transfer of sands onto the medicine-moistened hands of the singer. The sands are taken from the feet, legs, body, and head of each of the painted figures and then pressed on the corresponding body parts of the person sitting on the painting. When this identification is complete, the sand painting, badly defaced during the rite, is completely destroyed by the singer, who scratches through it with a plumed wand. The mixed sands are removed and returned to nature.

In the study of Navajo religion I have attempted to understand the significance of sand painting from the Navajo perspective. Each pattern is appropriate to only certain ones of the many Navajo ritual ways. Each has its own story of origin, which in turn is framed by the whole Navajo tradition of creation. I have found that no Navajo sand painting can be understood very well without placing it in these contexts. Every ritual performance is uniquely appropriate to the specific motivating circumstances which emphasize certain features of a given painting. While the attempt to understand any sand painting is a highly complex affair, I want to present a generalized interpretation here. A fuller analysis of a single sand painting will be presented in the following chapter, "Whirling Logs and Colored Sands."

In the ceremonials in which sand-painting rites play a major role, the cause of the illness being treated is attributed to impaired relationships with specific life-giving forces in the Navajo cosmos. These life-giving forces are associated with certain holy people whose powers have become directed against the life forces of the ailing person. In the ceremonial cure rites are enacted to appease the holy people and persuade them to remove their life-threatening influence. But this in itself does not constitute a cure, for the person must be placed again in a state of order modeled on the creation of the Navajo world. The sand-painting rite is therefore a rite of re-creation in which the person is remade in a way corresponding to the conditions of his or her ailment. In this rite of re-creation the sand painting is the essential vehicle.

The perspective of the person being re-created is based on his or her position in the center of the sand painting facing east, the direction of the road of life. This visual perspective on the painting is unique and cannot be shared by anyone. It is a view of the sand painting from within it, being surrounded by it. Only portions of the sand painting may be seen at any one time, and these only from the center outward. To sit upon the sand painting and to be identified with the many holy people and cosmic dimensions which are alive in it is to experience the complexity and diversity, the dynamics and the tensions, represented in the surrounding painting; but it is also to experience the one point common to all, and therefore to see and to feel the diversity and tensions.

The illness suffered is an experience of the world at odds with itself, but this experience is cosmicized when the person finds that this is but an incident in the whole drama of the universe. The illness is overcome when the person realizes (in the largest sense of that term) that in some places these tensions and oppositions can be balanced in a unity that signifies good health and beauty.

But how do we understand the destruction of the painting? We must see that it is not the materials of the sand painting, nor really even the design it takes, that is at the core of its meaning and power. Rather it is the process and use that is made of it that is important. It is a cosmic map. It is a vehicle by which re-creation, health, and beauty in life and the world are achieved. The sufferer finds his or her way to health from within the sand painting and by becoming a part of it; in turn it disappears and becomes a part of him or her. The picture disappears in the process of a person coming to know the fullness and unity of the reality it represents. The destruction of the picture corresponds to the dissolution of the tensions and imbalances that have given rise to the suffering.

We are now quite used to seeing Navajo sand paintings reproduced in books and articles on varying subjects. The circle inscribed by a cross is a widely known design, but its universal significance seems somehow shallow to me once I have considered Navajo sand painting, especially when I find that a fully closed border is rare and has very special significance and that double symmetry divided by a cross is but one of many general patterns.

The concerns I have are deepened as I begin to compare how we, as outsiders, view sand paintings with how Navajos view them, even from a physical perspective. Let me list several points of comparison. We have only representations of sand paintings drawn or painted on paper or canvas, which we enjoy as objects of art. Navajos strictly forbid making representations of sand paintings and they are never kept as aesthetic objects. Even the use of sand painting figures in the sand-glue craft has not met with the approval of most Navajo singers. Sand paintings must be destroyed by sundown on the day they are made. They are not aesthetic objects; they are instruments of a ritual process.

In terms of visual perspective we always view sand paintings from a position which would be directly above and at such a distance that the whole painting is immediately graspable, with each side equidistant from our eyes. This is completely impossible for Navajos. I got a laugh when I asked some Navajos if anyone ever climbed on the roof of a hogan to look at a sand painting through the smoke hole. When a painting six feet, or even larger, in diameter is constructed on the floor of a hogan only fifteen or twenty feet in diameter, the perspective from the periphery is always at an acute angle to the surface. A sand painting cannot be easily seen as a whole. The most important point of view is that of the person being cured, and this person sees the painting from the inside out because he or she sits in the middle of it. These differences are basic and cannot be dismissed. The Navajo view is inseparable from the significance which sand painting has for them.

I think we can say that for the Navajo the sand painting is not the intended product of the creative process in which it is constructed. The product is a healthy human being or the re-creation of a well-ordered world. The sand painting is but an instrument for this creative act, and perhaps it is the wisdom of the Navajo that it be destroyed in its use so that the obvious aesthetic value of the instrument does not supplant the human and cosmic concern. The confinement of our attention to the reproductions of sand paintings is somewhat analogous to hanging paint-covered artists' palettes on the wall to admire, not acknowledging that these pigment-covered boards are not paintings but the means to create them. There is a certain aesthetic value in artists' palettes, I suppose, but surely most would think of this action as foolishly missing the point.

While I am delighted at the increased interest in viewing artifacts from Native American cultures as objects of art, I cannot dismiss the implications that arise from this Navajo example. Our view of

Native American artifacts as art objects is a perspective the people themselves may not hold and sometimes explicitly reject. Our usual way of looking at these objects is stripped of the complex cultural views unique to the tribe which frames the significance of the artifacts. We often don't even know the physical perspective from which the object was intended to be seen. As a result the significance these objects have for us surely has little to do with their meaning for the people who created them.

If this were a problem only with Navajo sand painting it might ease my concern, but I think it in a significant measure holds true for any artifact not made for sale outside the culture. Some other examples will illustrate the point further.

Ted Brasser, of the Museum of Man in Ontario, studied the self-directed aspect of many Native American objects in the regions east of the Rocky Mountains.[2] He found that such things as moccasins, birchbark dishes, wooden bowls, effigy pipes, drums, woven bags, snowshoes, breechclouts, and pipe bags were commonly designed to be viewed from the perspective of the wearer or user. Moccasins, for example, have the design on the toe oriented to be seen by the wearer, not by those looking at moccasins worn by others. Craftspersons confirmed the intentionality of a self-directed orientation for many objects.

Brasser found that effigy pipes were used by the Iroquoian and Algonkian peoples as aides in the concentration of thought; that is, they were instruments of meditation. The pipe bowl bore the effigy of the guardian spirit or the familiar spirit of a shaman. It was so placed on the bowl that only when the smoker put the stem in his mouth did he come face to face with the representation of the spirit. Hence through smoking the pipe, drawing the tobacco smoke through the stem while concentrating on the effigy, the smoker gained power from his guardian spirit. Among the Sioux peoples Brasser found self-directed effigy pipes of a bear facing the smoker, which were used by shamans whose power to cure and benefit war parties was attributed to the spirit of the bear. In their ritual performances these shamans personified bears, wearing fur costumes and moccasins with bear paws attached.

Examples from Brasser's research throughout the whole area east of the Rocky Mountains could be multiplied, but my point is that there is ample evidence indicating that the meaning of the effigy pipe is inseparable from the act of smoking the pipe, from the relationship the smoker has with the spirit represented on the pipe. It is inseparable from what occurs during the hours of concentrated smoking of strong tobacco. The visual perspective is dictated by the use for which the pipe is intended. When not in use the pipes are not placed on display for aesthetic pleasures but carefully wrapped in their bags.

To cite another example, I have long been dissatisfied with our whole framework for attempting to understand Native American ritual drama. I am uneasy especially with our views of masked performances. Our words mask and impersonate suggest that these ritual processes are somehow artificial, illusions, enactments of something else which is being imitated or represented. I have been little comforted that these performances are described as reenactments of the events of the gods in the primal eras. I feel strongly that, rather than reenactments or dramatic performances, they are the actual creation of reality. I have been concerned with some aspects of this process in terms of rites of initiation. I would like to consider another aspect of this related to masks. In initiation ritual it is fairly common to have initiates look through the eye-holes of masks. I think we usually interpret this as a means of demonstrating to the initiates the unreality of the mask; that is, we consider it as showing that what the uninitiated think is a real being is actually only a personification. But I think we may be wrong here. Again it is a matter of perspective. I would suggest that the perspective from which one gains the fullest meaning of a mask is not finally by looking at it at all, although this is certainly an essential stage in the process. The full meaning is gained by looking through the eye-holes of the mask and seeing the effect it has on the world. That is why it is a privileged view of the initiated.

A couple of Hopi examples give this view some support. The Hopi Don Talayesva tells of a time when he portrayed a giant kachina in the Soyoko ritual proceedings, which are aimed at disciplining uninitiated children. These monstrous-appearing figures come to houses of misbehaving children and demand that the children be given them to eat. This forces the parents to bargain with the kachinas in order to save their children. The children's bad behavior costs the family a great deal in the physical goods they must provide to temporarily satisfy the awesome visitors, and this, along with the fear aroused by the kachinas, serves to encourage proper behavior in the children. Talayesva describes a time when he wore the mask of the giant kachina and enacted this ritual process. He played his part very well, with great effect on the children. That night Talayesva had a dream, which he describes:

> I was tired and restless, and dreamed that I was still a Giant Katcina arguing for the children. I reached out my hand to grab a child and touched him. [Touching a child is strictly warned against for fear of frightening a child to death.] The little one held up his hands to me, crying and begging to be set free. Filled with pity, I urged him to be a good child in order to free himself from the Giant Spirit. I awoke worried, with a lump in my throat, and bells ringing in my ears. Then I spat four times and decided that if I were ever the Giant again I would have a better-looking mask and speak in a softer voice.[3]

By looking through the mask from the inside out, its reality was reflected in the faces of the children.

The other example is a comment made by Emory Sekaquaptewa regarding the experience of performing as a kachina:

> I am certain that the use of the mask in the kachina ceremony has more than just an aesthetic purpose. I feel that what happens to a man when he is a performer is that if he understands the essence of the kachina, when he dons the mask he loses his identity and actually becomes what he is representing. . . . The spiritual fulfillment of a man depends on how he is able to project himself into the spiritual world as he performs. He really doesn't perform for the third parties who form the audience. Rather the audience becomes his personal self. He tries to express to himself his own conceptions about the spiritual ideals that he sees in the kachina. He is able to do so behind the mask because he has lost his personal identity.[4]

In this description of the experience Sekaquaptewa expresses the paradox of how one is at once enacting an impersonation and also transformed into what one is impersonating. It is described in terms of perspective. One best "sees" the reality one is oneself manifesting by wearing the mask; while looking through its eye-holes one gains a view from the vantage of the audience so as to be able to know the reality it presents.

There is an inevitable conclusion to be drawn from these examples. We can never fully appreciate some Native American objects we consider to be art without also appreciating the contexts in which they are produced. When our understanding of art is so heavily focused on objects, we tend to look in the wrong place for art. We find only the leavings or by-products of a creative process, never even realizing what is transparent to our view. We fail to grasp the inseparability of art and religion. I am reminded here of an essay by Amiri Imamu Baraku, formerly known as LeRoi Jones, entitled "Hunting Is Not Those Heads on the Wall."[5] In it he criticizes the aspect of Western art which he identifies as a worship of art objects. He feels that the price paid for this is the failure to appreciate the creative processes of art. In his view art objects are what is left over from the art process, and they have no more to do with art than hunting trophies have to do with the hunt.

The Native American examples I have given are related to this idea, but the case is even stronger because the aesthetic values cannot be separated from religious processes. A point of view commonly found in Native American cultures holds that reverence for objects which we might judge as being of artistic or religious value can become a kind of tyranny which stifles the full expression of ideas and the proper performance of religious acts. These acts themselves are creative in a primary sense: they define and shape reality; they literally make life possible. In light of this we should dissociate ourselves from the notion that for Native Americans art is a noun. We might prefer to adopt the term *arting* coined by Baraku, so that we can think of the art of Native Americans as a process of creating and maintaining life-giving relationships.[6]

Each year we are dazzled by the publication of beautiful books on Native American art and by stunning museum exhibits. I read the captions to the plates: "Painted Hide, Sioux, Lent by . . . ," "Mask, Tlingit, from the collection of . . . " The more elaborate identifications give a few descriptive notes, but since they are frequently drawn from publications of collectors who have little knowledge of the ethnography, they are often in error or severely inadequate.

When I find a plate depicting an object which is from a cultural context I know something about, I close my eyes and try to picture it in its living setting. Opening my eyes and focusing again on the object propped up with plexiglass or pinned against a completely blank background, I can't help feeling a little sick. While it is true that increasing interest in the aesthetics of what we call "primitive art" has provided an increasing interest in Native American artifacts as objects of art, I think we have done just about everything possible to remove the aesthetic and meaningful elements which they bore in the setting of their creation. And having done this, we find it impossible to appreciate them except in a relatively superficial way.

A few—all too few—publications about the art of Native Americans overcome the sterilization process which strips the cultural contexts from the objects. Outstanding among them is Edmund Carpenter's *Eskimo Realities*. The objects which we consider as art pieces are placed in the milieu of Eskimo world sense not simply through verbal description but through the visual effects achieved by this beautifully crafted book (regrettably no longer in print), which leads to the conclusion:

> The concept "art" is alien to the Eskimo, but the thing itself, the act of art, is certainly there, carefully implemented as a dimension of culture. It is not, however, always easy to recognize. The Eskimo don't put art into their environment: they treat the environment itself as art form.
>
> Such art is invisible: it belongs to that all-pervasive environment that eludes perception. It serves as a means of training his perception upon the environment.[7]

Carpenter's book helps demonstrate this lesson of perspective I have been talking about. The shape of our own reality may blind us to the perspectives of others. Dominant objects from our perspective may, to the makers of those objects, be the leavings of a creative process completely invisible from where we look. What appears to us as an uninteresting background may be to others the ground against which reality gains orientation and human meaning. What we must first realize is that there are many ways of looking; then, that understanding is shaped by where you put your eyes.[8]

NOTES

1. Washington Matthews, "Mythic Dry-Paintings of the Navajos," *American Naturalist* 19 (1885):931-39.
2. Ted Brasser, "North American Indian Art for TM," in *The Religious Character of Native American Humanities*, ed. Sam Gill (Tempe: Department of Religious Studies, Arizona State University, 1977), pp. 126-43.
3. Don C. Talayesva, *Sun Chief: An Autobiography of a Hopi Indian*, ed. Leo W. Simmons (New Haven: Yale University Press, 1942), p. 184.
4. Emory Sekaquaptewa, "Hopi Ceremonies," in *Seeing with a Native Eye*, ed. Walter H. Capps (New York: Harper & Row, 1976), p. 39.
5. Amiri Baraku [LeRoi Jones], "Hunting Is Not Those Heads on the Wall," in *Home: Social Essays* (New York: Morrow, 1972), pp. 173-78.
6. Robert Thompson, in *African Art in Motion* (Berkeley and Los Angeles: University of California Press, 1974), and others have shown how true this is for African art.
7. Edmund Carpenter, *Eskimo Realities* (New York: Holt, Rinehart & Winston, 1973), p. 202. Another sensitive book introduced by Carpenter is Bill Holm and Bill Reid, *Indian Art of the Northwest Coast: A Dialogue on Craftsmanship and Aesthetics* (Seattle: University of Washington Press, 1975).
8. The phrase "It's where you put your eyes," was taken from a Sesame Street song.

Whirling Logs and Colored Sands

This chapter will focus on a single Navajo sand painting done in an actual ceremonial performance—the Whirling Logs sand painting of the Nightway ceremonial.[1] I will view several dimensions of the sand painting rite, considering its construction, the rite performed upon it, elements in the greater ceremonial context, and the associated stories. I am seeking to understand sand painting as much as possible from the perspective of Navajos and to illustrate aspects of Navajo religious thought.

In preparation for the construction of the Whirling Logs sand painting the center of the ceremonial hogan is cleared and the fire is moved to the side. A layer of clean sand is spread upon the floor and smoothed out with weaving battens. The sand painters make a guide for long straight lines by snapping a taut string to make an indentation in the sand base. The sand painting is constructed from the center outward under the direction of the singer, who does not usually participate in the sand painting. For the Whirling Logs sand painting, first the black cross which represents the whirling logs is constructed upon the center, which may be formed by burying a shallow bowl of water so that its surface is even with that of the painting. The center represents the lake upon which the logs float. The logs are outlined in red and white. The crushed colored materials used in making the sand painting are held in bark containers.

As the last arm of the cross is being completed, the roots of the corn plants which appear in each of the four quandrants are drawn, with their beginning in the central representation of the lake. Navajos have said that this is so because the corn needs water in order to live. The corn plants constructed in each quadrant are of four colors—white, yellow, blue, and black. Each is outlined in a contrasting color. Two ears of corn are shown on each stalk.

On each of the four arms of the whirling logs sit two *yé'ii*, or masked holy people. The outer figures are male and wear helmetlike masks with two eagle plumes and a tuft of owl feathers. They carry gourd rattles and spruce branches. The inner figures are female carrying spruce branches in both hands.

When the inner portion of the sand painting is complete, *yé'ii* figures are drawn adjacent to the ends of each of the arms of the cross. To the west is *hashch'é ooghwaan*, or Calling God, who is dressed in black and wears a blue mask ornamented with eagle and owl feathers. He carries in his hands a black wand decorated with representations of feathers of turkeys and eagles. The skins of blue birds are depicted as being attached to the wand. The figure on the east side is *hasch'éłti'i*, or Talking God. He is dressed in white and wears a white mask decorated with eagle feathers tipped with breath feathers and a tuft of yellow owl feathers, with a fox skin under the left ear. He carries a gray squirrel-skin pouch on a string. His eye and mouth markings are distinctive, but the sand-painting representation does not include the corn symbol on the face, as does the mask of the impersonator.

The *yé'ii* to the north and south are *ghwą́ą́'ask'idii*, or Humpbacks. They wear blue masks with a zigzag line of white lightning around them and red feathers representing sunbeams radiating out from the masks. The masks are topped with blue horns which identify them with mountain sheep. The hump on the back is a representation of a sack laden with goods. These *yé'ii* carry black staffs. The anthropomorphic rainbow guardian figure circumscribes the painting on all sides but the east. Plumed wands, which represent holy people, are erected around the periphery of the sand painting.

In the hands of the rainbow guardian are placed cups of herbal infusion, which will be used in the sand-painting rite. A cedar twig is laid upon the shell cup with which to administer the medicine. This completes the construction of the sand painting.

The Nightway ceremonial during which this sand painting is made is performed according to a Holyway-type ritual process. This indicates that it is performed for a person suffering a predicament whose cause is attributed to one of the *diyin dine'é,* or holy people of the Navajo. The ritual process is bent on reestablishment of proper relationships between the one over whom the ceremonial is being sung—the one-sung-over—and certain of the holy people. The expected results of these renewed relationships are that the malevolence will be withdrawn and the person may then be rightly remade or re-created. The sand-painting rites take place on the fifth through the eighth days of a nine-night ceremonial. It should be noted that Nightway is one of the ceremonials in which the holy people make their appearance by means of masked impersonators.

When the rites on the sand painting are about to begin, the one-sung-over enters the ceremonial hogan, and the singer or medicine person begins the whirling logs songs. The one-sung-over, carrying a basket of cornmeal, stands to the east of the painting and sprinkles cornmeal upon it. This gesture of blessing is repeated on the south, west, and north. Then meal is scattered all around the periphery. While the one-sung-over prepares to enter the sand painting, a *yé'ii* enters the hogan whooping and proceeds to sprinkle the picture with the herb medicine using the cedar twig. The application of medicine is done systematically and carefully. The one-sung-over enters the sand painting and sits down. The *yé'ii* approaches him or her with the shell cup of medicine from which he or she drinks. Some of the medicine is put on the hands of the *yé'ii,* and with this moisture he picks up sands from the feet, legs, body, and head of each of the figures in the sand painting, including the cornstalks, and applies them to the corresponding body parts of the one-sung-over. After each application, the *yé'ii* lifts his hands toward the smoke hole. When the application is completed, the *yé'ii* yells twice into each ear of the one-sung-over and leaves the ceremonial hogan. The one-sung-over then leaves the sand painting. The plumed wands are removed, and what remains of the picture is carefully erased by the singer using a feathered wand. The sand painting materials are taken out of the hogan to be correctly disposed of. The Whirling Logs songs are sung until the *yé'ii* departs.

The stories of Nightway are too extensive and complex to recount in detail. The principal story is about four brothers and a brother-in-law who go on a hunting expedition. The next-to-youngest brother is the protagonist and he is a visionary. His name, *Bitahátini,* means "his imagination" or "his visions." The story begins with a conflict between the visionary and his brothers because they do not believe the authenticity of the vision experiences and refuse to listen to *Bitahátini*. The two eldest brothers and the brother-in-law leave for a hunting trip, and the visionary decides to follow them the next day. While camping by himself he overhears a conversation between two groups of crows in humanlike forms. He learns that his brothers have killed a crow, a magpie, and twelve deer. Since the crow and magpie are the owners of the deer, the crow people decree that the brothers will get no more game. The next day the visionary catches up with his brothers and tells them what he has heard. Only the brother-in-law listens to him. The elder brothers continue to hunt for several days, but the visionary's prophecy proves correct; they get no more game. On the way home mountain sheep are spotted and the visionary is sent to kill them. As he attempts to do so, he finds that he is unable to release his arrows, and he shakes violently. He makes several attempts until finally the sheep reveal to him that they are really holy people. They are Fringe Mouths in disguise, and they give him the guise of a mountain sheep and take him into a canyon. The place to which he is taken is no ordinary canyon, and here the Fringe Mouths enact the archetypal performance of Nightway and teach *Bitahátini* its songs, prayers, and procedures. In an attempt to help recover their lost brother the elder brothers have left offerings of jewels and pollens in baskets at the cliff edge. These are used in the ceremonial performance.

During the performance the visionary is captured by *hasch'é ayói*, or Superior God, and taken to his home in the sky. Talking God is dispatched on a journey to recover the visionary. The ceremonial continues.

Finally, after testing the visionary's powers and his knowledge of Nightway songs and prayers, the holy people allow him to return to his home in order to teach what he has learned to the youngest of the four brothers. After the youngest brother becomes proficient in the ceremonial performances, *Bitahátini* disappears and it is believed that he has gone to live in the home of the holy people.

Washington Matthews, who studied the Nightway ceremonial for twenty years during the late nineteenth century, recorded a sequel to this story which he entitled "The Whirling Logs." In many ways it is a more complex and fascinating story than the other. The protagonist, once again, is *Bitahátini*, the visionary. Having seen the picture of the whirling logs when he learned the Nightway, he is driven upon a quest for the place of the whirling logs. The visionary prepares a hollow cottonwood log for travel down the San Juan River in search of this place. When he launches his vessel, it immediately sinks and *Bitahátini* fears he will lose his life. When they find that he is gone, his family seeks the help of holy people in finding him.

Upon rescuing him from the bottom of the river, the holy people ask what he was attempting to do. He reveals his desire to visit the place of the whirling logs and to learn of the mysteries there. His persistence overcomes the reluctance of the holy people to assist him. They prepare a hollow log with crystal windows and launch him down the river. Several holy people accompany his journey to keep him afloat in mid-stream and to assist him past obstacles. After a journey of many incidents the log enters a lake, and upon circling it four times lands on the south shore. The visionary is allowed to leave the log and enter the house of the Fringe Mouths of the Water, where he learns from them their sand painting. He reenters the log and it carries him around the lake four times again to land on the north shore, where another sand painting is revealed to him. Back in the log, he is carried out of the lake and along a stream leading to the whirling lake. Landing on the south shore, *Bitahátini* finally sees the whirling logs upon the lake. The story says, "He beheld the cross of sticks circling on the lake. It did not move on its own center, but turned around the center of the water. The log which lay from east to west was at the bottom; that which lay from north to south was on top. On each of the logs, four holy ones were seated—two at each end. . . . Many stalks of corn were fixed to the log."[2] As he watches, the log cross lands on the west shore, and the holy people who were transported by it enter a house. The visionary proceeds along the shore toward the west and he too enters the house. The holy ones are prepared for him and already have placed the picture of the whirling logs upon the floor. They reveal to him the rites of the painting. The visionary is then given a ride around the lake on the cross of logs with the holy people.

Taking his leave the visionary starts back to the south shore, where he had left his log vehicle, but on the way he discovers an area which would make a good farm. His pet turkey whom he had left behind appears there and produces seeds of four colors of corn and many other plants from various parts of its body. The turkey protects and comforts *Bitahátini*. The seeds are planted and grow to maturity in four days. Holy people appear to help with the harvest and to instruct the visionary on how to harvest, cook, and eat the foods he has grown. They build him a house and perform a harvest ceremony.

Left alone the visionary soon becomes lonely, yet he is reluctant to leave his stores of food behind in order to return home. Again the holy people assist him by spreading clouds upon the ground and wrapping his foods in them. This makes several small bundles which he can easily carry home. His journey is made upon a rainbow, and he is escorted by Talking God, Calling God, and Water Sprinkler.

After his return he teaches his younger brother the mysteries of the whirling logs so that his knowledge of Nightway will be complete, and he divides the vegetables and grains among his relatives for use as seeds. The story explains that before this heroic venture the Navajo people had no corn or pumpkins.[3]

An outstanding feature of these stories, which accounts for the tension and drama in them, is the existence of two kinds of worlds very different from each other. In the Nightway story there is the world of hunters and the game animals, and there is the world of holy people and the owners of the game. In the whirling logs story there is the world of the visionary's home and family, and there is the mysterious world of the holy people and the whirling lake. From the very beginning of both stories it is clear that the drama is focused upon the visionary because he has some knowledge of both worlds, while other Navajos apparently have little or no knowledge beyond their mundane world. As they unfold, the stories follow similar patterns. The visionary leaves the world of ordinary reality and travels to the other world, where he acquires knowledge. In the end he returns to relate this knowledge to those left behind. It seems that the holy people are free to visit the world of ordinary reality, but it is unusual and difficult for an earth surface person to visit the homes and world of the holy people. During the arduous journeys the visionary enters dangerous territories; he undergoes difficult tests; he suffers imbalance and fear. Yet as a result of his journey he gains knowledge, courage, and balance. Through him knowledge of the other world comes to the Navajo people. This knowledge often reveals facts basic to the subsistence of the Navajo people. It shows that the elements of sustenance—game, corn, and other foods—are ultimately owned by or dependent upon the world of the holy people. The journey of the heroic visionary provides a means by which a complex multidimensional reality as established in the story is integrated and unified.

It is notable that the holy people keep the pictures which are the models for sand painting on *naskhá*, a cloth or spread, sometimes specified as a cloud. During the archetypal performance these cloths are spread upon the floor for use and later folded up. In revealing the pictures to *Bitahátini* the holy people explain, "We will not give you this picture; men are not as good as we; they might quarrel over the picture and tear it, and that would bring misfortune; the black cloud would not come again, and rain would not fall, the corn would not grow; but you may paint it on the ground with colors of the earth."[4] In another place the visionary is told, "Truly they [Navajo people] cannot draw a picture on a cloud as we do; but they may imitate it, as best they can, on sand."[5] Here too the existence of two kinds of worlds and of two kinds of peoples is emphasized.

This double imagery is interwoven dramatically throughout the sand-painting ritual. The hogan in which the sand painting is constructed is blessed at the outset of the ceremonial and set apart from the world outside. The ceremonial hogan is identified with the hogan in which the world was created and consequently with the very structure of the universe. The sand painting, done within this ritual enclosure and in the context of many other ritual acts, provides an identification with the events in the primal era when the heroic visionary lived. It replicates the picture revealed to him in the canyon where he learned Nightway and in the house of the holy people on the shore of the whirling lake. It also represents the whirling logs which he observed on the lake and upon which he rode with the holy people. The very shape and design of the sand painting echoes the shape of the hogan and the quarternary structure of the universe.

The design of the sand painting incorporates a complex dual imagery. On each arm of the log cross sit a male and a female *yé'ii*. By the very nature of the cross the quarternary division of the world along the cardinal directions, east and west, north and south, is given representation. The paired Humpback *yé'ii* are set across from one another, as are Talking God and Calling God. The Navajo colors—white, blue, yellow, and black—are set across from their complements in the cornstalks. Contrasting colors are used as outline.

The rainbow guardian and the arc of plumed wands erected around the painting never completely enclose the sand painting. It is through this opening that the one for whom the ceremonial is performed enters and through which the *yé'ii* enter and leave. This is essential to the purpose of Navajo sand-painting rites and to the very meaning of the Navajo word for sand painting, *iikhááh*, which means "they enter and leave." This entryway, sometimes flanked by painted guardian figures, is aligned with the entryway of the ceremonial hogan, which faces east. This suggests that the Navajo recognize an essential communication and interdependence between the ritual world created in the ceremonial hogan and the ordinary world outside. This is precisely what the stories have shown in a different way.

Stylistically, something may be said about the way in which the double imagery is presented. In the story the log cross is contained within the lake, while in the sand-painting representation it projects out of the lake, reaching into the enclosed sphere. This seems to expand the significance of the log cross to more global dimensions and to suggest that it is not limited to the sphere of the lake. Still, the major holy people stand beyond it and control its movement with their staffs. The corn plants which appear in the four quadrants are rooted in the lake from which they are nourished, but they project into the areas of each quandrant, thus also forming a cross joined at the center in the lake. The details of the story correspond closely with the structure of the sand painting. The revelation of the whirling logs painting and the origin of agriculture are represented in the picture, one by the cross of logs, the other by the cross of corn. In the story the log cross on the lake was described as having stalks of corn affixed to it, which suggests an interrelationship between the whirling logs and the origin of agriculture. This interrelationship is maintained in the sand painting, for both crosses are based or rooted in the lake in the center.

The sand painting is, at one level, a visual reminder of the events in the story of a heroic adventurer who obtained knowledge of the Nightway ceremonial, who experienced the mysteries of the whirling logs, and who introduced agriculture to the Navajos. At another level the sand painting is a geometric projection of the essential pattern of order in the world.

The tension of the double imagery gains further complexity in the rite which takes place on the sand painting. The earth surface person walks upon the painting and sits amidst the holy people. This entry to the sand painting reenacts the visionary's journey in that it brings the two worlds together. A *yé'ii* enters the hogan and walks on the sand painting to administer the rite. The masked appearance is another instance of the coincidence or integration of the two worlds. The *yé'ii* offers to the one-sung-over the medicines that have been fed and applied to each of the holy people in the surrounding picture. Then with the aid of the moisture of the medicine on the hands of the *yé'ii*, the person being treated is ritually identified with each one of the holy people by being pressed at ritually designated spots on his or her body with sands from the corresponding parts of all of the surrounding holy people. This act of identification is described in a common prayer segment which goes:

> His feet have become my feet, thereby I shall go through life.
> His legs have become my legs, thereby I shall go through life.
> His body has become my body, thereby I shall go through life.
> His mind has become my mind, thereby I shall go through life.
> His voice has become my voice, thereby I shall go through life.

In this way the person is identified with the very forces of the universe. He or she becomes one with the sources of life.

It is too little to say that for the person involved this identification must be a very significant event. The position on the logs identifies the person treated with the hero as he was escorted on the primordial ride around the lake. The suffering person too can experience this mystery. While it may well be beyond all description, his or her experience surely must be related to the position in the center of the sand painting which corresponds with the center of the world. The visual perspective of one sitting in the center of a sand painting is unique. From this vantage only portions of the painting may be seen at any one time, and these only from the center outward and perhaps upward. This visual perspective introduces a depth and movement to the picture that cannot be enjoyed from any other place. The person being treated has a heightened experience of truly being at the center. And by being at the center of the sand painting, this map of cosmic dimensions, the person who perceives its cosmic design becomes the integrative element within it. In the person on the sand painting the complexly dual aspects of reality and their tension is resolved. To sit upon the sand painting and to be identified with its many elements is to experience the point common to all of them and therefore to see the unity and wholeness of the universe. The sand-painting event accomplishes a re-creation of the person and the universe. The world which may have seemed at odds with itself, experienced in the person as physical or mental suffering, is unified and reintegrated in the sand-painting rite, where it is acknowledged that the whole drama of the universe is repeated in the human being.

In the complex representation through the double imagery in the sand painting and the ritual acts, the person who is the subject in the ritual may achieve a unity transcending this duality, an integration of the many to the one. This opens to the person an experience of reality in which he or she may grasp the spiritual powers which are present in it and one with it.

In the sand-painting rite the person comes to experience the truth in the stories, which is that there are not two worlds, but one world composed of parts which are complexly interrelated and interdependent. Order and disorder (*hózhó* and *hóchó* in Navajo) are interdependent, as are health and sickness, life and death, spiritual and material.

Once this truth is experienced, the sand painting can no longer serve as a map. The person being treated has found his or her way from within the sand painting; as he or she has become a part of it, it has disappeared by becoming a part of him or her. With the experience of the unity of the world the sand painting, as a depiction of the order of the world, cannot exist. So the destruction of the sand painting that always occurs during its use corresponds with the dissolution of the double imagery it presents. When a person arises and leaves the sand painting, his or her experience of unity is confirmed in a way by the destroyed sand painting. The many colors have dissolved into one as the sands and the renewed Navajo person return to the world.

NOTES

1. For publication of the Whirling Logs sand painting see Washington Matthews, *The Night Chant, a Navajo Ceremony* (New York: American Museum of Natural History, Memoirs vol. 6, 1902), plate VI; James Stevenson, *Ceremonial of Hasjelti Dailjis and Mythical Sand Painting of the Navajo Indians* (Washington: Bureau of American Ethnology 8th Annual Report, 1891), Plate CXXI; Ruth Underhill, *The Navajos* (Norman: University of Oklahoma Press, 1956), p. 80; and Sam D. Gill, *Songs of Life: An Introduction to Navajo Religious Culture* (Leiden: E. J. Brill, 1979), Plates XXVa-XXXI.
2. Matthews, *Night Chant*, pp. 183-84.
3. *Night Chant*, pp. 171-97.
4. *Night Chant*, p. 165.
5. *Night Chant*, pp. 182-83.

Disenchantment:
A Religious Abduction

Some years ago I first observed portions of the ritual process by which Hopis initiate their children into their religious lives. I remember it clearly. It was early February, and the Hopi were celebrating the opening of their kivas and the return of the kachinas to the human world of the Hopi mesas. This occasion is Powamu, commonly known as the Bean Dance. Beans are planted and forced by the warmth maintained in the kivas to sprout early. The bean sprouting and the ceremonial events turn the attention of the Hopi toward the upcoming growing season.

The initiation of children accompanies Powamu. As I stood in the village of Mishong'novi, I observed groups of children, all decked out in new clothing and shoes, being instructed by their parents. These were the children being initiated into the kachina cult. Peering down one of the avenues between houses, I saw some of the children taken atop a kiva; one kachina held up a child's hands, while another whirled what appeared to be the cloth tassels of a sash gently against each child. The gentleness of this gesture belies the seriousness of the initiatory scenario of which it is a part. Were we to see the whole event, we would find that at least some Hopi children conclude their experience of initiation profoundly changed, bearing not the joys of conversion and revelation but rather feelings of betrayal and disenchantment. Hopi children are in a sense abducted from their childhood naïveté into maturity, and for us to consider more fully this initiatory process may open not only a deeper appreciation for Hopi religious practices, but also for widely used religious techniques.

The initiation into the kachina cult designates the formal beginning of participation in the myriad events of Hopi religious life. The rites of initiation are performed only once every several years during the annual celebration of Powamu, the first major winter ceremony in which the kachinas appear. Children around the age of ten enter the kachina cult by being inducted into either the Kachina Society or the Powamu Society. The rites of initiation into those societies vary somewhat, as do the privileges of the members, but both take place during Powamu, and until recently every child was initiated into one or the other. Most Hopi children still undergo this initiation.

Students of religion have recognized that initiation into the religious life occurs in a series of events that opens for our analysis the shape and meaning of a religion. The Hopi rites are commonly cited as a classic example. A careful scrutiny of the descriptive accounts of this particular Hopi initiation reveals that the interpretation usually given is limited and misleading. I will suggest an alternative interpretation based on the point of view that the ritual does what the Hopi say it does—that is, initiate the children into their religious lives by revealing to them the nature of the kachinas.

Description and Interpretations

The earliest description of the initiation version of Powamu I have found was written by Alexander M. Stephen at the Hopi village of Walpi, on First Mesa, in 1892.[1] The core of the ritual process, according to Stephen's description, takes place when the children are conducted into the kiva by their ceremonial fathers, whipped by Tungwup kachinas, and comforted by their mothers. Stephen advanced an explanation of this whipping rite that has been maintained by most other interpreters.

> The primary significance of the whipping (*wuvi'lauwû*) seems to be this: Until children have acquired some real intelligence or are, say eight or ten years old, they are made to believe that the kachina appearing at all celebrations are superhuman visitors, nor must such children even see an unmasked kachina. When they have grown old enough or are deemed to have sufficient understanding, then they are instructed that the real kachina have long since ceased their visits to mankind and are merely impersonated by men, but they must buy this knowledge at the expense of a sound flogging.[2]

Stephen revealed something in his interpretation that he did not mention in his description. He indicated that the initiation is for the purpose of teaching the children that the kachinas no longer come to the villages, but appear only through the efforts of impersonation which the children, as new members of the cult, may now begin to perform.

A problem for Stephen—indeed, the primary problem to which he spoke—was to explain what motivates the whipping of the initiates. He indicated that it is a kind of payment for the secret knowledge the initiates gain in the rites. Elsie C. Parsons, who undertook the task of editing Stephen's journal for publication, added a comment on the basis of her considerable experience, although it appears that she had not witnessed the initiation rites:

> The whipping of the children is interpreted by our Journalist [Stephen] as a kind of expiation in advance for learning about the kachina. It is no doubt a ritual of exorcism but possibly it is an exorcism for the children against the evils of life and to promote growth and well being.[3]

Parsons places both the Hopi and Stephen within Judeo-Christian categories of meaning. Stephen's journal actually says nothing of atonement. Parsons' introduction of exorcism, unfounded in the descriptive accounts she used, was perhaps based on her view that Powamu is generally a ceremonial focusing upon exorcism.[4]

Another description based on witness of the initiation rites prior to the turn of the century is that of Heinrick Voth, a Mennonite missionary at the Hopi village now known as Old Oraibi. Voth witnessed the initiatory form of Powamu in both 1894 and 1899. His account was published in 1901 and supplements the Stephen account. Voth described the whipping rite as separate from the initiates' education about the nature of the kachinas. He clarified the distinction between the Kachina and Powamu societies in terms of the rites of initiation and the privileges enjoyed by the initiated. He shed further light on the significance of the whipping rite with the following information:

> There is a tradition among the Hopi that this flogging ceremony was not always a part of the Powamu ceremony. It is stated that on one occasion a boy who had been initiated into the Powamu

fraternity had revealed the secrets that he had seen and heard. A council of the leaders of the fraternity was at once called and the question discussed as to what to do about it. All urged that a severe punishment be inflicted upon the perpetrator. Only the *kalehtakmongwi* (Warrior chief), now represented by Koyongainiwa, remained silent. After having been asked four times by the others as to his opinion about the matter, he first also expressed his displeasure at the occurrence and then suggested that the boy be flogged before all the other novitiates by Kachinas as a punishment and as a warning to the rest. This was done, and the custom was continued.[5]

Voth recorded the whipping as occurring on the sixth day of the nine-day Powamu ceremonial and indicated that the children are protected against seeing unmasked kachinas even after their whipping. According to Voth, it was not until the ninth night that the children learned that the kachinas were masked impersonators.

On this occasion the Kachinas appear unmasked, a very rare occurrence. The new Powamu and Kachina Wiwimkyamu (from Wimkya, member) that were initiated on the fifth and sixth days are to learn for the first time that Kachinas, whom they were taught to regard as supernatural beings, are only mortal Hopis.[6]

Stephen did not describe this event, but alluded to it two times by indicating that "the children are to be flogged this sunset in the court, after which they must not eat salt or flesh for four days, then they may look upon kachina and *wi'mi* in kivas."[7] *Wi'mi* are ceremonies.

Several witnessed accounts are available from the early decades of the twentieth century, but they add little to these earlier accounts.[8]

Descriptions and interpretations made through the 1930s placed major emphasis on the whipping rite.[9] The secondary literature has focused on this aspect of the initiation, maintaining with Stephen that the major information learned during the initiation is that the kachinas are masked impersonators rather than "real gods" as the children had been previously taught. Louis Gray, in the article on the Hopi in *The Encyclopedia of Religion and Ethics*, wrote, "Previous to this whipping the children have believed that the kachinas are real; after it they know that they are in reality only personifications." None of the secondary accounts raises the question of how this learning takes place, and not a single one gives any indication of how the Hopi children receive this knowledge.

It was not until 1942 that more was written about the effect the initiation has on the initiates. In that year the autobiography of the Old Oraibi Hopi Don Talayesva was first published. Talayesva had a vivid memory of his own initiation into the Kachina Society. He recalled,

> When the Kachinas entered the kiva without masks, I had a great surprise. They were not spirits, but human beings. I recognized nearly every one of them and felt very unhappy, because I had been told all my life that the Katcinas were gods. I was especially shocked and angry when I saw all my uncles, fathers, and clan brothers dancing as kachinas. I felt the worst when I saw my own father—and whenever he glanced at me I turned my face away. When the dances were over the head man told us with a stern face that we knew who the Kachinas really were and that if we ever talked about this to uninitiated children we would get a thrashing even worse than the one we had received the night before.[10]

This Hopi account emphasizes the shock experienced upon learning that kachinas are masked Hopi. The whipping is described as a device to ensure secrecy, a role consistent with the story recorded by Voth.

For her study of Hopi personality development Dorothy Eggan interviewed a number of Hopis about their experience of the initiation into the kachina cult. Her evidence shows that Talayesva's response is typical. She wrote that

> at initiation the child learned that the Kachinas were not *real gods* but merely representatives of them, and that they were an endless duty as well as a pleasure. The traumatic effect of this blow to a young Hopi's faith in his intimate world must be emphasized. All informants questioned by the writer have drawn the same picture of their reaction to initiation; their emphasis is rarely upon an anticipatory fear of it, nor upon the

physical hardships endured during it. Rather they stress a previous struggle against disillusionment in which the hints—not very specific because of the severe penalty for betrayal—of earlier initiates were dismissed; and finally the intense disappointment in and resentment toward their elders which survived in consciousness for a long time. . . . For Hopi children there was a double burden of disenchantment and modified behavior, for while an altered concept of the kachinas eventually became a vital part of their lives, excessive indulgence by their elders had disappeared never to return.

To exemplify this reaction Eggan quoted a Hopi woman as saying,

I cried and cried into my sheepskin that night, feeling I had been made a fool of. How could I ever watch the Kachinas dance again? I hated my parents and thought I would never believe the old folks again, wondering if Gods had ever danced for the Hopi as they said and if people really lived after death. I hated to see the other children fooled and felt mad when they said I was a big girl now and should act like one. But I was afraid to tell the others the truth for they might whip me to death. I know now it was best and the only way to teach the children, but it took me a long time to know that. I hope my children won't feel like that.[11]

On the basis of Hopi accounts it appears that the whipping is primarily an incentive for maintaining secrecy, but that the knowledge of the nature of the kachinas which is gained during the Bean Dance on the last evening of Powamu is experienced as a shocking disenchantment with the kachinas, Hopi ceremonials, and Hopi elders. This experience of disenchantment is vividly remembered throughout life.

Finally the most complete account based on an observed performance of the initiatory form of Powamu was written by Mischa Titiev. He and Fred Eggan were participants in the Powamu of 1934. Titiev's account clearly indicates the distinction between the whipping part of the initiation rite and the moment when the initiates learn about the kachinas. He describes the initiatory element of the Bean Dance, which is performed in the kivas on the ninth night of Powamu:

Then the dancers enter the kiva while one of their number stands by the hatch and calls down all sorts of jests at the expense of each man as he comes down the ladder. Inasmuch as the performers announce on entering a kiva that they are the real Katcinas, and as they are unmasked, it does not take long for the recent initiates to discover that the Katcina impersonators are their relatives and fellow villagers. In such dramatic fashion is the most important of all Katcina secrets revealed to Hopi children.[12]

More details of this witnessed event are available in Titiev's 1972 publication of his Hopi field notes as well as the description of the rites which he observed in 1954, with comments on the observed changes during that period of time.[13]

Given the disenchanting nature of the secret learned by the kachina cult initiates, it is certainly not surprising that they respond with shock and displeasure. What is more shocking to me is that none of the observers has shown the least surprise at the anomaly presented by these Hopi rites. Not a single observer has responded to the revelation of the secret of the masked nature of the kachinas with more than passive acceptance. But in light of the fact that the Hopi have been commonly regarded as being almost excessively religious—as evidenced by their constant involvement in religious activities—I feel that it is startlingly incongruous that Hopis introduce their children into their religious lives with the revelation that the kachinas are not real gods, but men dressed as gods. Should this not raise the question of the motivation and meaning of all of Hopi religious practices that are associated with kachinas? Does it not seem utterly in opposition to the abundant references which attest to the Hopi belief that the donning of a kachina mask transforms a man into a god?[14] And finally, it is hard to overlook evidence that the initiated Hopis follow with the utmost care procedures of deception calculated to bring about an experience of disenchantment. The mere fact of the intentionality suggests that there is more to it than appears on the surface. Hints of this significance are suggested in Eggan's report by the Hopi who said, "I know now it was best and the only way to teach the children." Certainly a major element in the meaning of the mature Hopi religious life must stem from this shock of disenchantment. And I would suggest this may hold true for students of Hopi religion as well as for the Hopi children.

Disenchantment: Death to Naïve Realism

The esoteric aspects of the kachina cult initiation will probably never be known to non-Hopis, but the surface structure of the events of the ritual of initiation suggests much.[15] Prior to their initiation the children meet the kachinas in the villages in a wide array of associated experiences. Some kachinas present gifts to the children, while others frighten and discipline them. In all contacts the children are carefully guarded against either seeing an unmasked kachina or gaining knowledge that the kachinas are masked figures. In this way the children are nurtured in a perspective of naïve realism; that is, they are treated in such a way as to support the adequacy of their commonsense view of the world. The children are raised to accept the kachinas exactly as they appear to them in the village, as spirit beings who have come to the village to overlook and direct human and cosmic affairs. They identify the kachinas with their physical appearances and actions.

During the kachina cult initiation rites the final development of the perspective of naïve realism is made through a period of intense contact with the kachinas. Children are acutely aware of the kachinas' presence in the village; they watch them move about the village; they may be whipped by them; they are told special stories about them; and they are given special gifts, which they are told are brought from the kachinas' home in the San Francisco Peaks. While the children perceive the kachinas as beings of a wholly different category than themselves, they are not separated from these powerful beings. They observe the interaction of the Hopi people with the kachinas when they visit their villages on many ceremonial occasions. Further, the children are taught that upon death a Hopi may become a kachina and return to work for the people.[16]

The nurturing of a perspective from which reality is viewed naïvely appears to lay the basis for the shock experienced at the conclusion of the initiation rite. This naïveté is shattered in the instant of realization that the kachinas are masked figures, impersonations perpetrated by members of their own village, even their own relatives. The loss of naïveté is always irreversible. The result, as is clearly indicated by Eggan's consultants, is that the reality of the kachinas, one's destiny, and the whole basis for reality are called into serious question. The interaction between the Hopi people and the kachinas, which the children had come to know as essential to the continuity of the Hopi way of life, appears now to be impossible. The kachinas are shown to be only disguised Hopi men, the relatives of the children, and not spirit beings at all. The disjunction between the kachinas and humankind, which had heretofore been rather easily bridgeable, has now become an abyss. And perhaps the most remarkable thing in light of the expected initiatory structure, the rites of initiation end on this note of discord.[17]

While the new initiates must enter their new lives suffering this disillusionment, the privileges enjoyed in their new status permit them to participate in the affairs they have found to be disappointing. They may now participate in kachina cult activities.[18] They may be present in the kivas during rehearsal and mask preparation activities. They are eligible to be initiated into secret societies, in which they may gradually come to know esoteric dimensions of the kachina cult. The initiation is constructed in such a way that a child's religious life begins in a state of seriousness and reflection, motivated by doubt and skepticism. The very nature of reality has become threatened. Each child must search out a new basis for perceiving a meaningful reality. There is tremendous incentive to listen more carefully to the stories of the old people. Don Talayesva describes his increased interest in these stories as stemming from his experience of initiation.[19] It is apparently through the stories and through participating in religious activities that new initiates find the meaningful equilibrium which gives them reprieve from the awful state of disenchantment. The kachina cult initiation is the formal introduction into the religious life of a Hopi, not the culmination of this life. It turns an individual from the nonreligious life and provides the motivation for seeking religious awareness.

Other Examples

Disenchantment is not an uncommon technique used to bring about the fundamental changes so basic to rites of passage. Other examples may be briefly described to show the extent and variety of this abductive force.

Australia: The Broken Bullroarer. The process of disenchantment can be seen at work in the initiation rites of the Wiradthuri tribes of Australia. The occasion is the initiation of boys into manhood. The boys to be initiated are abducted from the village, taken from their homes and their mothers. The rites are loaded with chicanery. The boys are commanded to walk with their eyes fixed on their feet so that they may not observe the staging of the trickery. A principal focus of the several rites rests upon the revelation of the nature of the spirit Dhuramoolan. The boys are told frequently that Dhuramoolan is coming near, and they are advised to listen for his approaching voice. They hear a whirring noise that grows louder and louder, but they do not know that the sound is being made by men whirling bullroarers (thin pieces of wood whirled at the end of strings). At a critical juncture in the rites the boys are covered with blankets and told that Dhuramoolan is coming and that he may eat them. With bullroarers speaking close by, the elders reach under each blanket and with hammer and chisel they knock an incisor tooth from the mouth of each boy. The boys think the spirit is taking their teeth while sparing their lives.

In this initiation an illusion of the perceptual presence of a spirit is prepared, and it is fully accepted by the initiates. But, the initiation culminates in a disenchantment of this knowledge. On the last day the boys are covered with blankets and a crackling fire is built. The bullroarers are whirled nearby, and the boys are told that Dhuramoolan is going to burn them. When the boys become very frightened, the blankets are removed from their heads, and they are shown for the first time the men whirling the bullroarers. Thus they learn that this artificial noisemaking is what they have taken to be the voice of Dhuramoolan. Pointing to the men whirling the bullroarers, the head man shouts, "There he is! That is Dhuramoolan!" and he explains to the boys how the noise is made by whirling flat pieces of wood on strings. Then the boys are given the bullroarers to examine; they may even whirl them. They are forbidden to tell the uninitiated about them or ever to make a bullroarer except during the initiation rites. Then they destroy the bullroarers by splitting them into pieces and driving them into the ground, or sometimes by burning them.

There is little information about how the boys respond to this revelation, but clearly they can never again be terrified as they once were by the voice of the bullroarers. Nor can they retain the naïve knowledge of Dhuramoolan's nature engendered in them during the initiation rites. They have learned that the world is not always as it appears to be. They must now come to terms with the spiritual nature of the figure Dhuramoolan.[20]

Africa: the Killing of Kavula. A striking example of the defamation of sacred objects in the initiatory process occurs in the rites of initiation into one of the healing cults of the Ndembu of Africa. As we would expect, the revelation of the nature of Kavula, the spirit of the healing cult, is an essential part of the initiation. But the process by which the initiates learn of Kavula is startling. The adepts prepare a frame made of sticks covered with a white blanket to represent the divinity. It is called *isoli.* One of the initiated hides beneath the blanket to play the part of Kavula. The initiates are chased by the adepts, caught, interrogated with unanswerable questions, taunted for being unable to supply appropriate answers, and eventually led to the *isoli.* The initiates are instructed regarding the formal procedure of greeting Kavula. When they address the spirit in the *isoli,* its voice returns their greeting. The initiates approach the structure and, when instructed to kill Kavula, they beat the object with the butts of their rattles. With each blow "Kavula" shakes convulsively, as if dying. The initiates are then led back to the village. When they enter it, an adept takes a firebrand, strikes it violently on the ground, and cries out, "He is dead!" After a brief closing oration the initiation is concluded.

Victor Turner, who reported these events, elicited comment on the killing of Kavula from the Ndembu people. Muchona, a knowledgeable old man, said, "Kavula is killed to frighten the candidate. For he believes he is really killing Kavula. He has been instructed by the adepts that 'If you see the spirit of Kavula, you must consider this is a spirit which helps people.' . . . The adepts are just deceiving the candidates at *isoli.*" One of the female initiates told Turner that it was "Kavula's back that we saw in *isoli.* When Kavula was killed the spirit flew away into the sky, not to Nzambi (the High God), but 'into the wind.' It could come again."

In this initiation rite the adepts use techniques of deception to build an illusion, a fictitious conception of reality, for the initiates.

Bringing the initiates into Kavula's sacred presence, they confuse them with unanswerable questions, tell them to kill the very spirit that is to be revealed to them, and assure them at the conclusion of the rite that he is dead. Once the rites are over, the initiates are even shown the construction of the *isoli*. The illusion is disclosed; the enchantment with *isoli* is broken. Kavula, as presented to them, is shown to be nothing but a blanket-covered framework of sticks. Remarkably, however, the initiate domonstrated in her comments on the event that she discovered in it something of the mysterious nature of Kavula. She came to realize that Kavula is not limited to his appearance in the *isoli*, but is something more. Somehow in the process she gained the knowledge that Kavula is a spirit that flew "into the wind" and can come back; or perhaps, as Munchona told Turner, "Kavula takes all powers." It is through the creation of an illusion that is subsequently shattered by a dramatic and powerful act of disenchantment that the revelation of the spiritual dimension of reality is effected.[21]

Disenchantment: The Birth of the Religious Perspective

In these examples from Australia, Africa, and North America the whole process of initiation builds to a climax in the shock of disenchantment. The ritual objects are destroyed or their ordinary character is revealed to the eyes of the initiates. Despite this, the initiations evidently succeed, although the revelation of the religious or the spiritual is as much a result of the initiatic process as a part of it.

When the dynamic of disenchantment is the driving power in an initiation rite, the first and essential ingredient is encouraging identification of the spiritual with some physical/sensual aspect of the world. The uninitiated must come to believe that the objects and entities observed are what they are presented as being. The white blanket in the framework of sticks *is* Kavula; the masked dancers *are* Hopi spirit beings; and the roar of the noisemakers *is* Dhuramoolan shouting. Ingenious techniques of secrecy and deception have been devised to nurture a perspective of naïve realism, and the effectiveness of the initiation depends on how firmly this viewpoint is established.

The whole initiatory process reinforces this sense that the fullness of the religious reality is invested in these figures and objects. Then in the concluding moments, upon the threshold of a new life, the illusion is dissolved, and the shock of disenchantment shatters all that went before. The experience makes a return to the previous state of life impossible. The naïve realism of the uninitiated perspective has been exploded. The rites have demonstrated irreversibly that things are not simply what they appear to be, that one-dimensional literalism is a childish faith that one has to grow beyond or else despair of a life rich in meaning and worth. Surely, being thus forced to abandon one's ingrained notion of reality is to experience a true death of the former self. And this loss of self constitutes the concrete transformation signified by the death experienced in the rites.

The purpose of initiation—to reveal the fullness of reality—is, of course, one with the nature of religion itself. For religion springs from the unique human capacity to grasp and to create dimensions of reality that are beyond the material, beyond the obvious, beyond even human existence, and to exercise this capacity by utilizing the material and obvious dimensions of ordinary human life.

Through initiation culminating in disenchantment, the novice is in a sense abducted into the religious life in a state of crisis, disappointment, or perplexity about the nature of reality. The only thing he knows is that he has been fooled and his sense of what is real and what is not is confounded. His options seem clear. He may see the world as meaningless, or he may undertake a quest for a fuller understanding of the world. This is scarcely a choice. The experience of disenchantment initiates the world-creating and world-discovering human and cultural processes we know as religion. It stimulates inquiry, thought, creativity, wonderment, and the eventual formation of the sense of the religious world. The newly initiated are invited and expected to participate in the religious activities of their communities. Through such participation they begin gradually to grasp the full scope of the reality that their initiatory experience has opened for them. With this expanding awareness, meaning may once again be conferred on the defamed objects, yet now in an enhanced and mature way.

The profound wisdom of the method of initiation by disenchantment lies in its capacity to bring the initiate through succeeding stages of perception to an encounter with a fuller reality. The rites necessarily must end on the threshold of revelation, for it is only through the living of the religious way that the nature of reality becomes fully known.

Conclusion

Following Victor Turner, who discussed the Gospel story of the empty tomb along with the killing of Kavula events, I too would like to briefly consider this biblical story, for I believe that this story of death and resurrection also involves the enchantment-disenchantment process at work in the initiation of the Christian tradition.

The Gospels recount the life and teachings of Jesus as the story of the incarnate revelation of God. The episode of the empty tomb concludes the books of Matthew, Mark, and Luke, and in John only one chapter follows it. It comes directly after the account of the crucifixion, and for those destined to be members of the first Christian community this death caused fear, despondency, and consternation. This is especially clear in the concluding words of the Gospel of Mark:

> And very early on the first day of the week they [the two Marys] went to the tomb when the sun had risen. And they were saying to one another, "Who will roll away the stone for us from the door of the tomb?" And looking up, they saw that the stone was rolled back—it was very large. And entering the tomb, they saw a young man sitting on the right side, dressed in a white robe; and they were amazed. And he said to them, "Do not be amazed; you seek Jesus of Nazareth, who was crucified. He has risen, he is not here; see the place where they laid him. But go, tell his disciples and Peter that he is going before you to Galilee; there you will see him, as he told you." And they went out and fled from the tomb; for trembling and astonishment had come upon them; and they said nothing to any one, for they were afraid.

If we consider this as the concluding event in the initiation of the first Christians, several elements are remarkably similar to the rites of initiation described above. As the Ndembu experienced the death of Kavula, the Hopi the unmasking of the kachina figures, the

Wiradthuri the destruction of the bullroarers, so the followers of Jesus were forced to witness his death. They had come to know him well and had accepted him as their Lord. Yet they saw him captured, tortured, and crucified. They saw that he was a man who felt pain, suffered, and died. He, like any man, was placed in a tomb. The followers of Jesus had embraced a naïve view of his realty—that Jesus the man and Jesus the Christ were simply identical. But going to the tomb, they found that he was not there. The Ndembu who examined the *isoli* found only a framework of sticks—Kavula was not there. The Hopi found only their own relatives under the masks—the kachina spirit beings were not there. The Wirandthuri coming from under their blankets found only men whirling bullroarers—Dhuramoolan was not there.

The story of the empty tomb in Christianity follows a pattern akin to the abducting process of disenchantment. Christianity as a religion begins with the empty tomb which is received not with joy and comfort, but with trembling, astonishment, and fear. That which had appeared to be so real, the man Jesus, had ceased to be, and not even his body remained as an object to care for and reverence. It has been in the face of the fear and astonishment at the loss of Jesus, the man, that Christians throughout the Christian era have been led to grasp the reality of Jesus, the Christ, who was resurrected from the tomb, and hence the reality of God. It must follow that only with this revelation could it be clearly recognized that it is the life and teachings of Jesus that are the "living and the momentous revelation of the inexplorable" God.

In these few examples from a broad spectrum of religious contexts there appears the common structure of a technique of disenchantment used to initiate the process of developing the mature religious perspective and to promote authentic apprehension of the fuller nature of reality. The apparent effect of disenchantment is itself illusory. Acts which seem to spell the end of religion are the very techniques that thrust the initiate into the arena of adult religious life with incentive to plumb its full depths. They lay bare the limitations of naïve views of reality so that through deepened participation in a religious community and celebration of the day-to-day events of life in religious ritual, the individual may increasingly explore, create, and experience worlds of fuller meaning.

NOTES

1. It is not clear how much of the full initiation sequence Stephen observed. In Parsons' introduction to Julian H. Steward, "Notes on Hopi Ceremonies in Their Initiatory Form," *American Anthropologist* 33 (1931): 56-79, she indicated that Stephen had not seen the whipping rites in 1892, yet the account in his journal (*Hopi Journal of Alexander M. Stephen*, ed. Elsie C. Parsons [New York: Columbia University Press, 1936], pp 198-202) certainly appears to be written on the basis of direct observation.
2. Stephen, *Journal*, p. 203.
3. Stephen, *Journal*, p. 156.
4. Parsons presents an extensive comparative discussion of the whipping practice in her, *Pueblo Indian Religion* (Chicago: The University of Chicago Press, 1939), vol. 2, pp. 467-76, including various Pueblo peoples. Stephen's journal was not published until 1936, but an account based solely on his notes was published by J. Walter Fewkes, *Tusayan Kachinas*, Bureau of American Ethnography 15th Annual Report (Washington D.C., 1897). Since Fewkes had not witnessed the initiation form of Powamu, he added nothing to Stephen's notes.
5. H. R. Voth, *The Oraibi Powamu Ceremony* (Chicago: Field Columbian Museum Publication 61, Anthropological Series, vol. 3, no. 2, 1901), p. 105.
6. Voth, *Oraibi Ceremony*, p. 120.
7. Stephen, *Journal*, pp. 198, 202.
8. In Frank Waters, *The Book of the Hopi* (New York: Viking Press, 1963), pp. 176-79, an account of the kachina cult initiation is given as described by White Bear based on the 1914 initiation rites at Old Oraibi. The odd feature of this description is that it appears that the children see the dancers in an unmasked appearance before they undergo the whipping rite. When Waters describes the Bean Dance which concludes Powamu, he remarks, "All initiates know by now that the kachinas are mere men who impersonate them, and have full knowledge of Powamu" (p. 182). In Elsie C. Parsons, *A Pueblo Indian Journal* (Menesha, WI: American Anthropological Association, Memoirs no. 2, 1925), the account of the initiation into the kachina cult is described by the Hopi Crow-Wing, who mentions the whipping and the appearance of the Powamu kachinas as being without masks, but does not connect either very closely with the initiation. Steward presents a witnessed account on First Mesa from his field notes in 1927, but it does not add to the earlier accounts and does not make

clear when the children learn the nature of the kachinas. Steward indicates that the audience for the Bean Dance was "made up entirely of women who bring children, even small babies" ("Notes on Hopi Ceremonies," p. 71), but he does not make clear that only the initated children and very small babies may be present.

9. For examples of this emphasis see Louis Gray, "Hopi," *Encyclopedia of Religion and Ethics* ed. James Hastings (New York: Scribner's, 1920), 6: 783-89; Erna Fergusson, *Dancing Gods: Indian Ceremonials of New Mexico and Arizona* (Albuquerque: University of New Mexico Press, 1957), pp. 128-29; Walter C. O'Kane, *Sun in Sky* (Norman: University of Oklahoma Press, 1950); p. 185; and Alan W. Watts, *The Two Hands of God: The Myths of Polarity* (New York: Braziller, 1963), p. 206.

10. Don C. Talayesva, *Sun Chief: An Autobiography of a Hopi Indian*, ed. Leo W. Simmons (New Haven: Yale University Press, 1942), p. 84.

11. Dorothy Eggan, "The General Problem of Hopi Adjustment," *American Anthropologist* 45 (1943): 372.

12. Mischa Titiev, *Old Oraibi: A Study of the Hopi Indians of Third Mesa* (Cambridge: Paper of the Peabody Museum of American Archaeology and Ethnology, vol. 12, no. 1, 1944), p. 119.

13. Mischa Titiev, *The Hopi Indians of Old Oraibi: Change and Continuity* (Ann Arbor: University of Michigan Press, 1972), pp. 341-43.

14. See Titiev, *Old Oraibi*, p. 109.

15. For descriptions of these events see Titiev, *Old Oraibi*, p. 118; Stephen, *Journal*, pp. 224-27; Voth,, *Oraibi Ceremony*, p. 118; E. Earle and E. A. Kennard, *Hopi Kachina* (New York: J. J. Augustin, 1938), Plates X, XI; J. Walter Fewkes, *Ancestor Worship of the Hopi Indians*, Smithsonian Annual Report for 1921 (Washington, 1923), Plates 2, 7, and "On Certain Personages Who Appear in a Tusayan Ceremonial," *American Anthropologist* 7 (1894): 32-53. Emory Sekaquaptewa, "Hopi Ceremonies," in *Seeing with a Native Eye*, ed. Walter H. Capps (New York: Harper & Row, 1976), pp. 35-43, has a particularly clear description of the view Hopi children develop toward kachinas.

16. This belief, which is alluded to by Eggan's consultant, is documented throughout Hopi literature.

17. The "betwixt and between" state of liminality as described by Arnold van Gennup, *Rites of Passage* (Chicago: The University of Chicago Press, 1901) and extensively explored by Victor Turner, *The Forest of Symbols: Aspects of Ndembu Ritual* (Ithaca: Cornell University Press, 1967), esp. chapter 4, may be applicable here. But instead of concluding the initiation by establishing a new equilibrium to resolve the state

of liminality endured throughout the initiation process, it appears that it is the state of liminality that the children are being initiated into by these rites. A related discussion of liminality as associated with the Zuni ritual clown is presented by Louis Hieb, "Meaning and Mismeaning: Toward an Understanding of the Ritual Clown," in *New Perspectives on the Pueblos,* ed. Alfonso Ortiz (Albuquerque: University of New Mexico Press, 1972), pp. 163-95.

18. Titiev, *Old Oraibi,* p. 116, and others have indicated that children do not normally begin participating to any great extent for several years after their initiation.
19. Talayesva, *Sun Chief,* p. 85.
20. R. H. Matthews, "The Būrbŭng of the Wiradthuri Tribes," *Journal of the Anthropological Institute of Great Britain and Ireland* 25 (1896): 295-317; A. W. Howitt, *The Native Tribes of South-East Australia* (London: Macmillan, 1904), pp. 516-63.
21. Victor Turner, *Chihamba the White Spirit: A Ritual Drama of the Ndembu,* Rhodes-Livingstone Paper no. 33 (New York: Humanities Press, 1962).

"And he took away their wings":

Story and History in American Folk Traditions

"And he took away their wings"—a provocative phrase from a Native American story. It stimulates our curiosity, invites our attention. Despite such phrases that pervade Native American story traditions, we have yet to pay much attention, to attribute much significance, to the story traditions of aboriginal and folk Americans. The Native American teller of the story from which this phrase is taken would have understood our failings, for, you see, in his story, it was *our* non-native wings that were taken away.

In this chapter I will consider two story situations. Both European-Americans and Native Americans were involved in these situations. My objective is to investigate the dynamics, the efficacy, of the story genre, of the storytelling event, of the spoken word, and especially the interrelationships between story and history. I wish to move beyond the naïve and ill-informed notions that stories are merely entertainment or fanciful fantasies. I hope to move beyond the more elevated attributes of "myth" as charters for society and as educating devices. I do not deny that stories are and do these things. But it seems to me that in looking at stories from such a ground-level vantage, we miss the vitality and creativity of stories we might see had we the wings to gain an elevated view.

The story situations for our present concern are ones of encounter. They are two of the thousands of clashes that composed a disharmonic symphony of incongruity that played its way westward across the United States during the period of American history. Its echoes can be heard still, but now more softly. The brutality, the inhumanity, the bloody raw ugliness of these encounters are now muted and sometimes made harmonic by the stories of the encounters, the stories by which these encounters have endured.

Tecumseh and General Harrison

The first story focuses on the early-nineteenth-century encounter of two powerful figures—General William Henry Harrison, then governor of the Indiana Territory, and the Shawnee warrior and native spokesman and leader Tecumseh.[1] The political and historical background to their meeting is long and complicated, but the issue that divided them, yet brought them to encounter, may be summarized in a single word—land. Land had been the central issue since the time the first European placed his foot firmly and irretrievably upon this continent. Story after story might be told to document the shift of land from Native Americans to European-Americans, and in the early nineteenth century the land story came to focus on the real estate bordering the Wabash River in what we now know as Indiana. By treaty with various Indian chiefs in 1805 prime land along the river was opened to settlement. Tecumseh, who was not a part of these treaty negotiations, insisted on his right to the land under the principle he so often and so clearly stated: that the land belonged to no single Indian or tribe, but rather, if it could be said to be owned at all, it belonged in common to all Indian peoples and therefore could not be sold without the consent of all Indian peoples. Throughout the first decade of the nineteenth century Tecumseh traveled constantly and widely among the tribes in an attempt to form an alliance among them to repel the advancement of American settlement. The Wabash was the last stand east of the Mississippi and south of the Great Lakes.

Harrison was an ambitious man. Indeed, his ambitions led him to the presidency. As governor of the territory and administrator of Indian Affairs, he was personally involved in treaty negotiations for lands. Tecumseh's refusal to vacate the land and the threat of the alliance that he was forming disturbed Harrison. In his efforts to resolve the matter, Harrison invited Tecumseh to meet with him in Vincennes, the territorial capital. The meeting was set for mid-August, 1810.

Accompanied by three hundred painted warriors floating down the river in eighty canoes, Tecumseh made a grand entrance at Vincennes. He camped just outside the town and spent several days preparing for the meeting with the governor. Meanwhile, Harrison, who had built a governor's mansion called Grouseland, prepared it for the meetings. He arranged seating on the portico of the mansion and invited dignitaries to be present during the meetings. On August 14 Tecumseh, accompanied by a number of armed warriors, approached the mansion. After some negotiations regarding the physical arrangements for the meeting, opening speeches were made by Tecumseh and Harrison. They continued to meet until August 21.

No agreements were made. Harrison and Tecumseh not only spoke different languages, they lived in different worlds. They held conceptions of land and land use whose only point in common was the physical land itself. This meeting, though colorful, was unremarkable and would not seem to be of interest to us now. But the meeting became the setting for a story; a story that appeared in several versions; a story that was told widely throughout a good portion of the nineteenth century; a story that has played a surprising role in the history of scholarship; a story that has made its mark on the history of Native American religions. I'll get to these things, but first the story.

One version of the story appeared in Henry Rowe Schoolcraft's *Travels in the Central Portions of the Mississippi Valley*. Describing the character of Tecumseh, Schoolcraft recounted the story.

> The spirit and fearless energy of this man's character shone throughout his actions. In one of the councils held by General Harrison with the Indians at Vincennes, previous to the commencement of hostilities in 1811, in which Tecumseh was present, this chief, on concluding a long and animated speech, found himself unprovided with a seat. When this neglect was observed, General Harrison directed a chair to be placed for him, and requested him to sit down. "Your father," said the interpreter, "requests you to take a chair." "*My* father!" replied the haughty chief, "the *Sun* is my father, and the *Earth* is my mother, and on *her* bosom I will repose." So saying he sat down suddenly, in the Indian manner.[2]

I have located nearly thirty published and manuscript accounts of this story. They may be sorted into several clearly distinguishable versions. All, however, contain a statement attributed to Tecumseh and presented as an exact quotation: "The earth is my mother and on her bosom I will repose."

I want to consider this story in light of what we can document as history so that we might understand more fully the dynamic interrelationship of story and history. Important to our consideration is that the story is not an Indian story; it is a story about an Indian.

Notably, the first published appearance of the story was in 1821 in the *National Recorder,* followed by the account published by Schoolcraft in 1825. Evidence suggests the story was widely told in Indiana when Schoolcraft visited there in 1821. When the eyewitness and historical accounts of the meeting are considered, those that appear before the 1830s do not make the slightest allusion to the famed statement of Tecumseh. Even after that date there is commonly only a brief reference to the statement among the historical accounts. In the histories the basic concern with the initial meeting at Vincennes is with the negotiation and political maneuvering of the parties present. The published stories of Tecumseh's remark to Harrison reflect and evidence what I would call a folkloric strain. These story accounts do not consider to any extent the historical details of the meeting, yet they invariably cite the meeting as the historical setting for the story. They invariably tell the story to demonstrate the character of Tecumseh.

Weighing all available materials, I have concluded that there is absolutely no documentation of any kind for Tecumseh having made the statement about his desire to repose upon the bosom of his mother, the earth. Upon a careful review of the many speeches of Tecumseh that have survived and of what is known of Shawnee religion and culture at the time, I have further concluded that there is very little possibility that Tecumseh would have held the notion of earth-sky parentage either in a theological or metaphorical sense. Nothing remotely associated with it can be found in any of these historical materials.

What then accounts for the genesis of the story? What was the function and significance of the story? We need consider more about Tecumseh and the history of the Indian-white affair.

After Tecumseh met with Harrison in 1810, he immediately left for a long journey among southeastern tribes to continue his efforts at developing an Indian alliance. Harrison, doubtless encouraged by Tecumseh's absence, engaged the Indians at Tippecanoe in the battle for which he became so famous. Upon his return Tecumseh saw that the Indian cause was lost unless, through alliance with the British, the Indians could recover the territory from the Americans. Therefore, Tecumseh and other Indians played an active role in the War of 1812. During these many campaigns, Tecumseh proved his character, his military genius, his skill at leadership, his courage and bravery in battle.

In 1813, in battle against his old adversary Harrison, Tecumseh was killed. His body was never found. The mystery of his death accented a fascination that grew around Tecumseh. He was quickly and widely lauded as a noble Indian, a great leader and eloquent spokesman for peoples who had become landless and downtrodden.

At this particular moment in this history of conflict we glimpse something vital to human life: the dynamic process in which history engages the imagination driven toward the creation of meaning through the formation of story, a story expressible by that most magical of all human capacities, the power of the spoken word. The story of Tecumseh is an American story, and examining the interrelationships between history and story reveals to us something of our own character.

What is important is how the Harrison-Tecumseh story functions in the context of history. It reflects and effects a change in the image held of Indians, a change from an image of them as a savage people so void of rights and brains that their lands may be taken from them for a token payment or by military force, to an image of them as noble people of natural dignity, honor, courage, leadership, and eloquence. The story reflects, and doubtless helped to effect, a change in attitude toward native peoples; a change easily made once these peoples were either dead or without any claims to the coveted American lands. To appreciate the nobility of Indians by lauding the characters of a few outstanding leaders and figures was widespread in America in oral traditions widely told after the War of 1812, and in literary accounts beginning in the third decade of the nineteenth century and persisting for decades.

The story is told as history by its association with a historical event and historical figures, and therefore it is validated and authenticated. Yet, knowing that the story is not historically factual, we may see that the story actually serves to interpret history. The story corrects history by atuning past events to perceptions and sensitivities current to the time of the storytelling. The story makes history by presenting a new and different image of Indians, authenticated by its documentation in a past event. No longer bloodthirsty savages murdering innocent settler families, the Indians become figures capable of nobility, dignity, intelligence, and humanity, traits based on a simple and natural primitiveness, traits that flow from the bosom of the earth. A more surprising impact I believe this story has had must await our consideration of the second story situation.

Smohalla

In Tecumseh's time, the early nineteenth century, the Indiana territory was part of the Northwest Territory of the United States. Little more than half a century later, despite a civil war, the symphony of incongruity had played across the continent all the way to the territories of Washington and Oregon, the new Northwest Territory. This movement west was remarkably fast and decisive for American and Native American history.

With marked resemblance to the plight of Tecumseh in this new northwest area there is the famed story of young Chief Joseph, who led his people on a failed flight to freedom. We know well the stories of Joseph and his peoples, his famous utterances, and less so the brutality of the encounter. We scarcely are aware of the pathetic end of his life in Oklahoma. Joseph was not permitted to return to his homeland. While there are stories here for us to pursue, Joseph is not my present concern. Rather, I wish to consider another Indian figure in this territory, Smohalla, a Wanapum man, who led a few followers in the defiance of the government's effort to confine Native Americans in the Washington-Oregon area to reservations so that settlement of their aboriginal lands might proceed.[3] Smohalla was not simply a renegade leader; he was a religious leader. The movement he led was known as "the dreamers." It was millenarian in character, anticipating the catastrophic end of the world; an end when all Americans of European descent would be eliminated and the ancient ways of the native peoples would be restored along with the lands that had been taken from them. Perhaps, had it not been for the potential military aspect of this movement, the government might have made no effort to resolve the incongruity it posed. But in the mid-1880s Major J. W. MacMurray was sent to attempt to persuade Smohalla and his people either to go onto reservations or to take up settlements of land.

MacMurray was courteously received by Smohalla and his people, who invited him to observe the rituals of the dreamers. Finally, given his turn, MacMurray produced a checkerboard as a visual aid in describing the settlement plan and how the government wanted the land divided. He urged the Native Americans to apply for land and to settle it on the pattern of European-Americans. Smohalla responded that he could not accept this and proceeded to tell his story of the creation of the world. It is this story of Smohalla's that I wish to consider more fully. As MacMurray reported it, the story goes this way:

> Once the world was all water, and God lived alone; he was lonesome, he had no place to put his foot; so he scratched the sand up from the bottom, and made the land and he made rocks, and he made trees, and he made man, and the man was winged and could go anywhere. The man was lonesome, and God made a woman. They ate fish from the water, and God made the deer and other animals, and he sent the man to hunt, and told the woman to cook the meat and to dress the skins. Many more men and women grew up and they lived on the banks of the great river whose waters were full of salmon. The mountains contained much game, and there were buffalo on the plains. There were so many people that the stronger ones sometimes oppressed the weak and drove them from the best fisheries, which they claimed as their own. They fought, and nearly all were killed, and their bones are to be seen in the sand hills yet. God was very angry and he took away their wings and commanded that the lands and fisheries should be common to all who lived upon them. That they were never to be marked off or divided, but that the people should enjoy the fruits that God planted in the land and the animals that lived upon it, and the fishes in the water. God said he was the father, and the earth was the mother of mankind; that nature was the law; that the animals and fish and plants obeyed nature, and that man only was sinful. This is the old law.[4]

The story is set in primordial times and we would, therefore, call it myth, yet we cannot help but recognize Christian elements in the story and undeniable echoes of the native experience of oppression at the hands of white settlers. We cannot overlook how strongly the story pronounces judgment upon the oppressors and how punishment levied is linked to a policy about land use and ownership that could have come from the mouth of Tecumseh, a half continent away and nearly a century earlier. "And he took away their wings and commanded that the lands and fisheries should be common to all who lived upon them.'"

How does this story function in the context of history? Like the story about Tecumseh, this story interprets history. Smohalla and his followers had lived for decades with the experience of being buffeted by the tide of acculturation that had carried away most of the native peoples. This bleak, hopelessly irresolvable situation was woven into the story of creation. All the suffering of Smohalla and his people at the hands of the settlers, their loss of land, their loss of life, their loss of culture—these things are not denied in the story; rather they are affirmed, yet given meaning. Smohalla and his dreamers were living out a sacred history, and the story that gave direction and authority to their history gave them courage, dignity, strength, and hope. Further, the base of meaning is the firmest and most unquestionable of all, for this is the story of the creation, the story of the way God created the world and has participated in its history. God created the world, and the land, and he created plants, animals, and fish to feed the peoples. He created the people with winged freedom that they might move about the earth. But the strong oppressed the weak, and in his anger at the destruction this brought about, he took away their wings and commanded that land be held in common by all who lived upon it. This story not only reinterprets a history of suffered oppression, it establishes with divine and primordial authority a course of action, a way of living. It states an old law by which to give life meaning even upon radical change and in the face of suffering oppression and loss.

The Power of Story

We have then two stories. One was created by European-Americans about the encounter between themselves and Native Americans. The other was created by Native Americans about the encounter between themselves and European-Americans. Both reinterpret history so as to give it meaning. Both serve to create history not only in the reinterpretation of the past, but in the sense of providing a base, an authority, a course for the actions that open to the future. Both stories seek an unquestionable base for their validity and authority. For the European-American story this base is history itself. For the Native American story the base is the primordium and the creator, what we might call the authority of myth. This difference is fundamental, and through it we may learn much about Americans with European ancestry and about Native Americans.

In the past we have tended to make much of the distinction between history and myth or story, a difference parallel to literate and nonliterate, civilized and primitive. We have tended to take history seriously, to see it as our connection with reality and with our true past. We have tended to take story as fictive, imaginative, nonhistorical, and therefore not to be taken seriously, especially if it is the story of the folk. Our brief consideration of these two stories suggests that the careful distinction between history and story is fundamental and essential. Neither the story of Tecumseh nor the creation story told by Smohalla is historical, but history is behind and within both and it is essential that we identify the historical elements. Our examples show us that we cannot continue to make a host of assumptions on the basis of a genre distinction alone. We have found an important interdependence between story and history. Indeed, we might suggest that story is a manifestation of the power of the word to render history, and consequently human life, meaningful. History lacks meaning without story. Story lacks substance and relevance without history.

There is some sympathy and harmony between these two story situations, I feel, and it would not surprise me that if we knew more about the history of these two situations and the history of the development of Native American conceptions of the land, we might not discern some historical connection between Tecumseh and Smohalla. I am not the first to notice some connection between them, and that notice becomes the focus for yet another level of consideration of these two story situations.

First, however, to establish the basis for this further consideration we must take the Smohalla encounter with Major MacMurray just a bit further. After Smohalla had told his story of creation to Mac-Murray, thereby establishing the "old law," he went on to comment on the course of action that was open to him and his followers based upon this law. As reported by MacMurray, Smohalla said:

> Those who cut up the lands or sign papers for lands will be defrauded of their rights, and will be punished by God's anger. . . . It is not a good law that would take my people away from me to make them sin against the laws of God. You ask me to plough the ground! Shall I take a knife and tear my mother's bosom? Then when I die she will not take me to her bosom to rest.
>
> You ask me to dig for stone! Shall I dig under her skin for the bones? Then when I die I cannot enter her body to be born again.
>
> You ask me to cut grass and make hay and sell it, and be rich like white men, but how dare I cut off my mother's hair?
>
> It is a bad law and my people cannot obey it. I want my people to stay with me here. All the dead men will come to life again; their spirits will come to their bodies again. We must wait here, in the homes of our fathers, and be ready to meet them in the bosom of our mother.

These are the famous words for which Smohalla has been remembered. Still, we cannot understand their power or their meaning without comprehending the history of oppression and loss of land and without knowledge of his story of creation. Based in the old law of creation, this statement responds to the oppressive demands of European-Americans that Native Americans give up their cultural ways and take up farming and mining, that they participate in the division of the lands. Smohalla holds this to be sinful, that is, a violation of the laws of creation and the laws of God. He constructs his statement upon the metaphor of the motherhood of the earth.

Seemingly coincidentally, but perhaps not, both the story about Tecumseh—a story made by Americans, I remind you—and the statement attributed to Smohalla include the distinctive reference to the bosom of the earth. Given the histories, contexts, and functions of these two stories, it is surprising to learn that they have been conjoined—we might say in the bosom of the earth—in yet another story.

As early as 1873, in his publication *Primitive Culture*, Edward B. Tylor cited the statement attributed to Tecumseh out of the story we have discussed as ethnographic documentation for his understanding that a belief in the motherhood of the earth was pervasive among the peoples of North America.[5] Shortly after the statement of Smohalla was recorded, it was conjoined with the Tecumseh statement as evidence of this religious belief in the earth as mother. James Mooney, in his widely known study of the Ghost Dance movement of 1890, made much of Smohalla's statement and created the following theological story. In his monograph, following directly upon the quotation of Smohalla's statement, Mooney wrote:

> The idea that the earth is the mother of all created things lies at the base, not only of the Smohalla religion, but of the theology of the Indian tribes generally and of primitive races all over the world. This explains Tecumseh's reply to Harrison: "The sun is my father and the earth is my mother. On her bosom I will rest." In the Indian mind the corn, fruits, and edible roots are the gifts which the earth-mother gives freely to her children. Lakes and ponds are her eyes, hills are her breasts, and streams are the milk flowing from her breasts. Earthquakes and underground noises are signs of her displeasure at the wrongdoings of her children. Especially are the malarial fevers, which often follow extensive disturbance of the surface by excavation or otherwise, held to be direct punishment for the crime of lacerating her bosom.[6]

The statements attributed to Smohalla and Tecumseh appear together as evidence for a theology of the native belief in the motherhood of the earth. Soon after the beginning of the twentieth century, corresponding roughly with Albrecht Dieterich's 1905 publication *Mother Earth*,[7] the goddess took on the formal title of Mother Earth and was widely compared with the earth goddesses of Western antiquity.

In a careful review of the ethnographies and studies of the religions of tribes all over North America, I have found evidence of many goddesses. Some are associated with the earth, associated in a variety of ways; and I have also found many others that are not. The religion and cultures of the early-nineteenth-century Shawnees share little with the religion and cultures of the late-nineteenth-century Sahaptan peoples of the Plateau area. There is simply not a shred of evidence to support the commonly proposed statement of the ancient and universal belief in a mother earth goddess among tribal peoples in North America.

What we must conclude from this consideration is, once again, the creative power of story. With the need for common categories of comparison, with certain primitivist assumptions being fostered in the post-Enlightenment, strongly evolutionist mood of the late nineteenth century, scholars interpreted the information they received relative to Native Americans and by means of the power of words bestowed meaning upon the data by rendering them in terms of a story. It is a story that has been told again and again in the scholarly community by such figures as Mircea Eliade and Åke Hultkrantz.[8]

The last twist should demonstrate finally the power of story and its interaction with history. As Native Americans began to lose their land base and thus their connection with the tribal histories and tribal identities, they had need, and desperately so, for some firm footing in a shared tradition. Taking on the name by which European-Americans had always called them, they began to call themselves, identifying their commonality, by the term *Indian*. They further accepted the story told by European-American scholars of their ancient universal goddess, Mother Earth, and in their acceptance she begame a true goddess central to the Indian identity. She gave a religious grounding to an essentially political movement. Mother Earth as a goddess arising in the twentieth century nourishes and maintains a distinctively Indian heritage when physical lands are no longer available. She serves in many ways to make Indians clearly distinct from non–Native Americans. Here the story becomes history, and, ironically, a native story tradition of Mother Earth is practically nonexistent.[9]

In these examples we have histories that become stories—stories that interpret, even alter, the historical facts, yet become the basis for the unfolding of history. There are stories of history and histories of story. We must never blur or neglect the distinctions between story and history; rather, we must appreciate the dynamic interaction and interdependence of story and history. Life experience, the past, oppression, incongruity, suffering, and joy all gain meaning, they take wing, through the power of story, through the magic of words.

NOTES

1. For a full bibliography to the history of Tecumseh's encounter with Harrison as well as the story traditions that are associated with it, see Sam Gill, *Mother Earth: An American Story* (Chicago: The University of Chicago Press, 1987), chap. 2.
2. Henry Rowe Schoolcraft, *Travels in the Central Portions of the Mississippi Valley: Comprising Observations on Its Mineral, Geography, Internal Resources, Aboriginal Population* (New York: Collins & Hanney, 1825), pp. 144-45.
3. For a full bibliography to the dreamer movement led by Smohalla see Gill, *Mother Earth*, chap. 3.
4. J. W. MacMurray, "The 'Dreamers' of the Columbia River Valley, in Washington Territory," *Transactions of the Albany Institute* (Albany, 1887), pp. 247-48.
5. Edward B. Tylor, *Primitive Culture* (London: John Murray, 1873), 1: 326-27.
6. James Mooney, *The Ghost Dance Religion and the Sioux Outbreak of 1890*, Bureau of American Ethnology 14th Annual Report (Washington, D.C., 1896), p. 721.
7. Albrecht Dieterich, *Mutter Erde: Ein Versuch über Volksreligion* (Berlin-Leipzig, 1905).
8. See Gill, *Mother Earth*, chap. 6, for a full review of the scholarship on Mother Earth.
9. See Gill, *Mother Earth*, chap. 7, for an account of the history of Mother Earth as a goddess to Indian peoples.

Prayer as Performance:

A Navajo Contribution to the Study of Prayer

Frank Hamilton Cushing, ethnographer, lived at Zuni in the late nineteenth century. The Zuni accepted him and even made him a priest of the Bow society. A Zuni poem recalls the initiation of Cushing into the Bow priesthood.

> Once they made a White man into a Priest of the Bow
> he was out there with other Bow Priests
> he had black stripes on his body
> the others said their prayers from their hearts
> but he read his from a piece of paper.

There is a double edge to the humor of this poem, for in Zuni language the term used for the written page is "that which is striped," so Cushing, with his white body painted as a Bow priest with black stripes, was literally a walking page of writing.[1]

I think this poem gets to the heart of the criticism that can be made of the academic study of prayer. It distinguishes between a heartfelt act of prayer and a prayer formally recited from a piece of paper. The difference has yet to be adequately appreciated. This failure is clear when we see that the study of prayer has hinged upon attempting to reconcile prayer as it appears in the form of texts with the ideas we have about prayer that have been developed on the basis of personal experience and common knowledge. The study of prayer has been based largely on the analysis of written texts and shows prayer to be a formulaic, repetitive, redundant, and even trite verbal act. This conflicts with the expectation that prayer be a spontaneous, creative, and extemporaneous conversation human beings have with God about their heartfelt concerns. In textual forms prayers appear rigid and uncreative in contradiction to the expectation that prayers will be free and spontaneous.

Most students who have approached the study of prayer on the basis of a comparison of isolated texts have seen this difference as a problem, and they have been frustrated by their inability to resolve it. I have found, to the contrary, that this difference is not a problem that must be resolved, but rather it is a key to our understanding of prayer as a meaningful and efficacious human act. We are simply encountering the difference pointed to so nicely by the Zuni, the difference between text and act, the difference between prayer considered as constituted only by its words and prayer considered as constituted by a performance which engages aspects of utterance, including a wide religious and cultural context in association with the words.

Edward B. Tylor's ten-page discussion of prayer in *Primitive Culture* (1873) stands today as a classic statement, and it has been surpassed by very few studies of prayer. Prayer is a standard entry in phenomenological studies of religion, but here the principal concern has been to distinguish it from other forms of religious speech, especially magical spells.[2] Prayer is usually mentioned in general treatments of what has been called "primitive religion," but these vary little from Tylor's statement.[3] Other than Frederick Heiler's *Prayer* (1932) there have been no significant extensive comparative studies of prayer.

It is not of interest here to present fully and critically the history of the academic study of prayer, short as it is; but by briefly describing and commenting upon a few significant moments in this history I can highlight those features that have been consistently recognized as distinctive of the character of prayer. Notably, the very character of prayer is interlocked with the unresolved problems encountered in the study of prayer.

Turning Points in the Study of Prayer

Tylor and the Evolutionist Assumption. In the formative period of the fields of anthropology and the comparative study of religion, evolutionist and primitivist perspectives shaped the way that religious phenomena were seen and defined. The study of prayer is interesting in this historical context because the phenomena of prayer so clearly confused and confounded the assumptions on which were built this organization and understanding of religion.

Edward B. Tylor's discussion of the nature of prayer has greatly shaped the scholarly view of prayer since the late nineteenth century. It is not difficult to find Tylor's views on prayer in currently published works on exclusively oral peoples. He considered prayer to be the address of personal spirit to personal spirit. It is a conversation distinguishable from ordinary human speech acts primarily in that it involves a supernatural entity. Tylor agreed that prayer is "the soul's sincere desire, uttered or unexpressed," but when it is expressed, it is an act of intelligible speech in more or less ordinary language that addresses reasonable and practical concerns.[4] He held these characteristics of prayer to be incontestable because the nature of prayer is simple and familiar to us all. This was Tylor's view of prayer as a religious act of the heart.

The confoundment of Tylor's understanding of prayer arose when he considered prayer in the comparative study of culture, and especially as it confronted his evolutionist hypotheses. Here he dealt with prayers primarily as recorded and written texts, not as performed acts. Tylor considered prayers in both "primitive" and "advanced" cultures, but it was difficult for him to make distinctions between the prayers of these culture types in order to chart the evolution of prayer or prayer forms. The only evolutionary correlation he was able to advance was in terms of the ethical character of the message of the prayer. He posited that "primitive prayer" was concerned primarily with selfish personal needs and wants, while the prayer of "higher religions" took on ethical concerns to become an instrument of morality. Tylor probably knew that this would not withstand rigorous testing, but he held to his evolutionist view and despaired when the practices of more advanced cultures did not properly align with their attained level of advancement.[5]

While the content or message of the prayer text could be forced to yield, however disappointingly, to the evolutionist assumption, this was less possible when considering the formal character of ritual prayer. The highly structured and rigidly maintained character of prayers that contradicted Tylor's expectation of prayer as a spontaneous outpouring of the human heart was found to be as evident in "high religions" as in "primitive religions." Rosaries, prayer wheels, and formal liturgical prayers found throughout the world religions could not be ignored. This formal character of prayer posed a most difficult problem for both the definition of prayer and the evolutionist schema which sought to interpret it. Again, there was little choice but to yield the case as a failure and to attempt a recovery by pointing out what caused the failure. Ironically, Tylor suggested that the process of civilization was the culprit by forcing worship, and consequently prayer, into a mechanical routine needed to regulate human affairs by fixed ordinance. He wrote, "Thus prayers, from being at first utterances as free and flexible as requests to a living patriarch or chief, stiffened into traditional formulas whose repetition required verbal accuracy, and whose nature practically assimilated more or less to that of charms."[6]

The empirical data on prayer should have forced the evolutionist position into acknowledging a reverse case, a movement from religion to magic, prayer to charm. By Tylor's definition prayer is a speech act between man and god, but the processes of civilization undercut its basically communicative character by forcing it into becoming a formulaic act. Prayer became charm in the process of civilization. But at this point prayer and charm overlap and blur to the point that we can no longer distinguish them on the basis of the original definition that prayer is an intelligible act of speech. The content and, especially, the form of prayer when confined primarily to ritual text, to words, present a major problem to the evolutionist position.

Tylor's view of the effects of prayer is consistent with his intuitive understanding that prayer is a heartfelt and spontaneous communication between humans and higher beings: "Wherever it occurs prayer is a means of strengthening emotion, of sustaining courage and exciting hope."[7] Tylor stood with the Zuni in seeing prayer as an affair of the heart; but in his comparative studies of culture he approached prayer, as did Cushing, by limiting its scope largely to what was written on paper. By doing so he met with the disparity signaled by the Zuni response to Cushing.

Reichard and a Structural Approach. In the early 1940s a new period in the study of prayer finally began the departure from the position that had been stated by Tylor and carried on by Heiler,

Radin, Lowie, van der Leeuw, and others. Susanne Langer, in *Philosophy in a New Key* (1942), identified symbolism as the generative idea that was shaping the entire scope of the human sciences. Just two years later Gladys Reichard published a book on Navajo prayer entitled *Prayer: The Compulsive Word*. While this book is concerned only with Navajo prayer, it is important because of its approach to the interpretation of prayer. There are implications in Reichard's study that suggest a movement from the evolutionist perspective to a new symbolic and structural perspective. However, Reichard failed to develop fully this new perspective and settled on a view of Navajo prayer as mechanically compulsive.

By using alphanumeric designations she charted rhythmic word and phrase patterns in Navajo prayer texts. Once these patterns of repetition were charted, she proposed structural divisions corresponding with her interpretation of content. These distinctions in both form and content were made without explicit criteria, but several levels of structure were defined. At one level were distinctions such as invocation, petition, and benediction; at another level were distinctions such as address to the deity, the reason for the deity coming to the aid of the one praying, the symbols of the deity, the behavior of the deity, the concern expressed by the deity, and the description of repetitive ritual acts. At still another level Reichard attempted to correlate two major types of rhythmic patterns with the general purposes to which prayers in these types are addressed.[8]

The implications for a new turn in the study of prayer stem from Reichard's recognition that the formal composition of prayer texts is significant and that aspects of the structure correlate with the performance context. These propositions open the way to resolve Tylor's dilemma. Reichard's attention to the form of prayer texts suggested that even the structured character of formula, of repetition, of convention, was inseparable from the communicative functions. But beyond that her study suggests that these correlations may be extended to the performance of prayers, prayer acts—that is, prayers uttered in specific social, historical, religious, and ritual contexts.

Reichard's book on Navajo prayer has had little, if any, impact on the broader comparative and general study of prayer, doubtless because she held to the notion, despite what her study suggested, that Navajo prayer is basically a magical utterance, signaled boldly in the title of her book.

Other Points. Since Reichard's study others have studied prayer and related genres of religious language in the broader contexts of performance in culture. Some studies focus only on the code structures found in prayer. For example, in a study of Zuni speech acts, including prayer, Dennis Tedlock considered inflectional patterns as a code which signals aspects of the intent of the speaker.[9] At the other end of the spectrum S. J. Tambiah focused on the metaphorical character of magical language to demonstrate that complex messages may exist even in apparently nonsensical charms. But this approach tends to ignore much of the rigid and highly repetitive character of these speech acts.[10]

Another development that suggests a potential advance in the understanding of prayer arises from the illumination of the performative aspect of language by philosophers of language. To my knowledge this has been tentatively considered in terms of prayer only by Philip Ravenhill,[11] and I have incorporated the perspective in a study of Navajo prayer.[12]

Other analytic paradigms have been fruitful in the study of prayer. For example, Gary Gossen adapted Victor Turner's approach to the study of ritual symbols in his study of Chamul prayers.[13] By illuminating meanings at the exegetical, operational, and positional levels according to Turner's scheme, Gossen was able to point to certain sets of time-space cultural categories that are encoded in these ritual speech acts. But while he shows that Chamul prayers demonstrate these categories, he has no particular concern for the peculiar or distinctive character of prayer as a speech form, nor for the significance of prayer as a religious act.

Critique and Comment. The most striking fact is that in the past half century the general study of prayer has received little attention. This is in spite of the advancements in the study of language, speech acts, and religious language made in several fields. The existing studies of prayer have generally suffered from one or more of several problems. Prayer is viewed in only semantic terms, as a system of encoded messages. The rigid and repetitive form distinctive of prayer is ignored. Prayer is studied primarily as text separated from the religious, cultural, and performance contexts. Some studies consider only the form or structural character of the speech act or some aspect thereof and exclude concern for the content and its meaning. Other studies are concerned with prayer only as a medium of culture and are not interested in understanding the nature of prayer.

While the study of prayer remains undeveloped, the fact is that prayer is among the most peculiarly remarkable of religious phenomena. It is foremost, and undeniably, religious. It has not been taken nearly seriously enough by students of religion. Can we claim to know much about religion while having ignored such a central and crucial act as prayer?

Prayer Acts in Navajo Culture

The intelligibility of the language of Navajo prayer is one of its distinguishing features. It has few vocables, so common to Navajo song, and it can be clearly understood even in translation. Navajo prayers may easily be written down and translated into English. While the message of this prayer is directed toward a pragmatic concern, the language is not without poetic imagery and reference to oral traditions. Navajo prayer is highly formulaic, rigidly guarded against change, and recited without verbal interpretation, interpolation, or significant alteration. In the examination of texts of prayers there seems little challenge or difficulty in interpreting much of their surface-level message. It is even easy to move to a deeper level of significance and meaning in the prayers where we find that the structure and images bear interrelationships with the whole Navajo cosmic system of interacting dualities. These categories are encoded in the prayers in the designations of direction, color, time, sexuality, and geography. We can easily see that Navajo prayer images reflect cosmic and cultural values.

When we move beyond the words to consider the performance of prayer as religious act, we move well ahead in comprehending the power of Navajo prayer. Here story traditions, ritual, and cultural concerns must be incorporated into our analysis. Navajo prayers are performed as the central and most important acts in most of the many ritual processes which constitute the enormously complex ceremonials of the Navajo. Prayers are usually intoned in litany fashion by a singer (a medicine man or woman) and the one for whom the ceremonial is performed, with the voices slightly overlapping. They are usually performed with the one praying sitting in a ritual position with legs extended, facing east, head slightly bowed, and holding a ritual object in his or her hands. The intonement of prayers may take from a few minutes to an hour or more. Everyone present is familiar with the distinctive sounds of the intonation and the common phrases of prayer performances. Prayers are never intoned or spoken outside a context which Navajo tradition has defined as appropriate. To lead the litany recitation of prayer one must have properly learned the prayer and the accompanying ritual and have cultural knowledge of the ceremonial way. In this way a Navajo gains possession of prayers.

Upon considering the semantic content of prayer texts in light of this simple description of the performances of prayers, there are notable observations to be made. First, while the message or information encoded in the prayers can be described at several levels, there is little indication that in the performance of prayers this information is particularly unique or informative, although it is not irrelevant to the situation. The style of the performance and the physical and emotional aspects of the performance seem to greatly overshadow any concern with message. Then, too, the immediate message is obvious to those present. Further, the message of the prayer is highly redundant due to dense repetition. The extent of repetition and the verbal elaboration of the prayers and the related ritual elements is greatly out of proportion to the extent of the semantic messages of the prayers. We must not ignore the obvious issue of why such complex and elaborate acts are required to convey a message so ill proportioned to these acts. We must ask why the information conveyed seems to be given such little attention. We must ask if there is not much involved in prayer that has little to do with the semantical referential meaning in the text. We must ask to what extent and in what ways prayer is more than a conveyance of encoded messages.

First, we must note that to any Navajo the sounds, the settings, and the occasions of prayer are distinctive. These elements signal that the act being performed is an act of prayer, thus framing it in the minds of Navajos. Thus they do not see a discrepancy between the referential dimensions of prayer messages and their knowledge of the ordinary empirical world. The performance characteristics of prayer permit Navajos to experience it as prayer, as an experience of the evocation of images which are capable of "strengthening emotion, of sustaining courage and exciting hope," as Tylor would have it. It is precisely because the performance of prayer signals that a special frame of experience should be engaged by those present that we can speak of prayers as being more than simply message-bearing in nature. Further, to explain prayers in terms of the simple semantical referential messages they bear is to ignore the question of why they are not simple nonredundant utterings of messages we can easily decipher.

Let me restate this in general terms, for I believe it applies not only to Navajo prayers but to prayers generally. Seen in one way, an act of prayer is clearly an intelligible communication between human beings and higher powers. It is a language act open to translation, interpretation, and analysis. But seen in another way, prayer is poetic in language and is performed as a highly complex ritual act. In this view whatever message exists in the prayer language is not nearly as important as its power to evoke a network of images related to sense experiences, moods, emotions, and values. This evocational aspect is borne not only in the form of rhythmic repetition and the language of the words but also, and perhaps to an even greater extent, in the context and texture of the ritual act of prayer—the sounds, sights, smells, stories, songs, ritual gestures, and dance movements that inform the experience.

A peculiarity of prayer is that it is both a practical and intelligible act of speech which seeks pragmatic results and a ritual act which engages and coordinates numerous contextual spheres in the creation of a network of rich images. While these aspects of prayer may seem disparate, they are in fact interdependent, for the performative dimensions of the prayer act serve its pragmatic concerns by engendering the powers of evocation which can transform moods, reshape motivations, muster courage, and present meaning-giving images. This means that while prayer is the communication of an intelligible message describing an expected pragmatic effect, the form in which that message is carried engages real processes which serve to achieve the desired results, even to the extent of physical cure.

Consequently we can see the possibility that the performance of a prayer act can be creative and responsive to heartfelt needs while being utterly formulaic. The creativity and immediacy of a prayer are not fully apparent at the level of its referential meaning, but they become so when a prayer is considered also as a religious act that incorporates much more than the isolated words of the text. In this wider frame it is virtually impossible to replicate exactly an act of prayer from one occasion to another, for the needs to which it speaks are always changing, as is the cultural milieu in which it is performed.

With this understanding of prayer it is clear that we must be able to analyze the referential meaning of the words of prayers but also to consider the meanings of the performative aspects of the prayer acts. We must analyze both the semantic content and the form of the prayer texts. But we must also be able to analyze a prayer as the performance of a religious act that is ritual in character, and we must be able to construct a description of the network of powerful images that the performance evokes. This will require the systematic analysis of the structures of a prayer in its context of ritual, oral tradition, and the specific circumstances motivating the particular performance of the prayer act.

What is thereby achieved is an understanding of ritual prayer as a religious act whose significance is achieved through a complex hierarchical set of structuring principles. When seen in a limited way, prayer has an internal tension between its pragmatic and its poetic and structural aspects. But when considered in the wider frame of performance, this internal tension is recognized as the source of its vitality and potency. Thus only when we extend the frame in which prayer is considered wide enough to include all of the dimensions its performance calls into play, but without losing track of the minute constituents in each of these dimensions, do we reach the point of achieving an adequate understanding of any prayer act.

The following interpretation of a particular Navajo act of prayer will demonstrate and illustrate this understanding of ritual prayer.

A Navajo Enemyway Prayer Act

On analysis of the structure of more than three hundred Navajo prayer texts, totaling more than fifteen thousand lines, in isolation from their performance context, I have been able to determine that all Navajo prayers are composed of combinations of some of twenty constituents that can be defined in terms of their content and poetic style. An analysis of the structure of all of these prayers in isolation from their performance contexts permitted the distinction of eight major categories of prayer. When the prayers were considered in their performance contexts, the classification of prayers correlated well with a Navajo ceremonial classification. This confirmed the hypothesis that the structure of prayer is significant. This can be demonstrated in the discussion of a specific prayer act.[14]

One class of prayer texts corresponded with the Navajo ceremonial classification Enemyway (*anáá'jí*), which is a ceremonial formerly used to respond to the infection caused by contact with foreigners—that is, non-Navajos—in the context of war, but is now used to respond to the problems of any infection believed caused by foreign contact. In either case the source of the malevolence is due to the agency of a foreign ghost—that is, the disembodied spirit of the dead foreigner.[15]

The following is a structural analysis of the Enemyway prayer known as the Prayer to Shoulder Bands and Wristlets. All Navajo ritual is modeled on the first performance of the ceremonial as told in an origin story. In the story of Enemyway this prayer is said on behalf of Young Man at Jarring Mountain, who helped the Corn People defeat the people of Taos. The prayer has twelve parts, each with a complex structure, but the constituent which distinguishes this prayer is concerned with the removal and dispersion of the foreign malevolence. The affliction being treated by the ceremonial and this prayer act is traced to the ghosts of defeated Taos enemies. This extensive prayer act is but a small portion of a four-day ritual process to treat the ailing Young Man at Jarring Mountain. The prayer is said in the context of a series of complex ritual acts to which it is associated.

As the preparation for these acts was taking place, animal figures came to the ceremonial hogan and contributed something to the medicine of Enemyway. Water was boiled, into which the medicine was put. Then the concoction was drunk from a basket by the young man. It worked as an emetic, and after he had vomited, the remainder of the medicine was applied to his entire body. The shoulder bands and wristlets, paraphernalia of war, were placed into his hands for the intonement of the prayer. After the prayer medicine was sprayed by mouth onto cotton strings. Slip knots were tied in these strings. The knotted strings were then held to various parts of the body of the ailing person and the knots pulled free. A black tallow was prepared by mixing burnt herbs into tallow, and the body of the young man was blackened with this mixture. All of these ritual acts were accompanied by song.

This archetypical performance of the prayer act and associated rites is used as a model for present-day performances of the prayer. Typically it would occur in the morning of the third day of a four-day (five-night) performance of the Enemyway ceremonial.

A consideration of this prayer act for the expulsion of foreign malevolence must include the emetic rite, the litany intonement of prayer, the unraveling rite, and the blackening rite. These rites when performed according to traditional prescriptions have the potential to evoke in a Navajo a network of images introduced through the story traditions and ritual performances. The imagery is also clearly articulated in the text of the prayer. As each rite is considered in turn, I will examine the images evoked by the rite and reinforced by the story which describes the motivation and precedents for the rite.

The Emetic Rite. Emetic rites are commonly associated with purgation. That has been the standard interpretation of this Navajo rite by scholars. But fuller examination of the Enemyway emetic rite reveals that the images it evokes are more complex. In the emetic rite the medicine is prepared in a Navajo basket, an object that in ritual is associated with unity, beauty, and health. The basket is placed on a figure of Ripener, a female insect figure who is strongly associated with fertility, that has been drawn on the floor at the rear (west side) of the hogan. On the surface of the medicine is drawn, in pollen, the figure of Big Fly, who serves as a messenger between human beings and the holy people who seldom come personally to the world of humans. Big Fly is a protector and informer. Pollen, of course, is invariably connected with health, life, fertility, and plenty. The emetic is drunk by kneeling with one's hands and knees on those of the figure of Ripener drawn on the floor. One drinks the medicine from the very center of the Big Fly figure drawn on its surface.

The songs sung during the preparation of the medicine identify it as food. "With a thrill, my grandchild, you have prepared a food for yourself, with a thrill . . ." And the songs sung during the application of the emetic medicine to the body of the one suffering identify him with Monster Slayer, who in primal times slew the monsters in order to make the earth's surface a place inhabitable by Navajos. The medicine is thus associated with the weapons and powers of destruction wielded by Monster Slayer in the killing of enemies.

The images evoked in the emetic rite cluster in two areas. One is distinguished by an emphasis on the expulsion of malevolence; the other by a concern for the acquisition of blessing—fertility, food, and life.

The Prayer Recitation. Immediately before the prayer is intoned, songs are sung. These are the songs that Changing Woman heard when her sons, Monster Slayer and Born-for-Water, returned from killing monsters. Changing Woman is a wholly benevolent figure in Navajo religion and is inseparable from the powers of creativity and life. She is time, motion, and creativity personified. The songs describe the achievement of a new order and happiness in the world because things have been put back into their proper places.

The shoulder bands and wristlets, the central ritual objects held by the one praying, are made of yucca. Their origin is told in the stories of Enemyway. When Monster Slayer killed one of the monsters he removed its colon, and filling it with blood he slung it across his shoulder. This initiated the practice of Navajo warriors collecting bloodstained articles from their enemies to display on their shoulder bands. Thus the objects are associated with the death-dealing powers and weapons of Monster Slayer as well as representing red trophies of victory over enemies and monsters. These are the instruments that helped put the Navajo world in order so that Navajo people might live in it.

The Prayer to the Shoulder Bands and Wristlets is a set of twelve prayers of identical constituency with two much shorter prayers appended. The first eight prayers name, respectively, Monster Slayer, Born-for-Water, Born at Yellow Mountain, Reared Underground, Sun, Moon, Talking God, and Calling God. These prayers differ from one another only in terms of the person to whom they are directed and certain alterations in line sequences and phrases.

The first prayer addresses Monster Slayer by the descriptive term "Who time and again kills monsters." It goes as follows:

Who time and again kills monsters,
He of "Waters flow together!"

His feet have become my feet,
  thereby I shall go about,
His legs have become my legs,
  thereby I shall go about,
His body has become my body,
  thereby I shall go about,
His mind has become my mind,
  thereby I shall go about,
His voice has become my voice,
  thereby I shall go about,
By which he is long life, by that I am long life,
By which he is happiness, by that I am happiness,
By which it is pleasant at his front, thereby
  it is pleasant at my front,
By which it is pleasant in his rear, thereby
  it is pleasant at my rear,
When the pollen which encircles sun's mouth
  also encircles my mouth, and that enables me
  to speak and continue speaking,

You shall take the death of the upright,
  of the extended bowstring out of me! You
  have taken it out of me, it was returned upon
  him, it has settled far away!
Therefore the dart of the enemy's ghost,
  its filth, by which it bothered my interior,
  which had traveled in my interior, which had
  absorbed my interior, shall this day return
  out of me, therefore I am saying this. Because
  this day it has returned out of me, I am saying
  this.
The dart of the enemy's ghost, its filth,
  by which it bothered my skin, which had traveled
  on my skin, which had absorbed my skin, shall
  this day move away from me, therefore I am saying
  this. Because this day it has moved away from me,
  I am saying this.

The dart of the enemy's ghost, its filth, has
turned away from me, upon him it has turned, far away
it has returned.
Right there it has changed into water, it
has changed into dew (while) I shall go about
in peace.

Long life, happiness I shall be,
Pleasant again it has become,
Pleasant again it has become,
Pleasant again it has become,
Pleasant again it has become,
Pleasant again it has become.

Prayers nine to twelve mention, respectively, the names White Corn Boy, Yellow Corn Girl, Pollen Boy, and Ripener Girl. These prayers are the same as the first eight except that the passage which identifies the one praying with the holy people has a variation in wording.

Where White Corn Boy . . . rests his pollen
feet, there I have placed my feet,
Where he rests his hands in pollen, there
I rest my hands,
Where he rests his head in pollen, there
I rest my head,
His pollen feet [legs, body, mind, voice] have
become my feet [legs, body, mind, voice], thereby
I shall go about [continuing as in the other
prayers].

Following the twelfth prayer two short prayers name Pollen Boy and Ripener Girl.

Pollen Boy,

Nicely you shall put my foodpipe
in its [former] condition again!
Nicely you shall put my windpipe
in its [former] condition again!
Nicely you shall put my heart
in its [former] condition again!
Nicely you shall put my nerves
in its [former] condition again!

Nicely I shall walk about, without ailment I
  shall go about, unaffected by sickness I shall
  be going about!
Without monsters seeing me I shall be going about!
Without beings which are evil seeing me I shall be going about!
With monsters dreading me I shall be going about!
With monsters respecting me I shall be going about!
Governed by this I shall be going about!
After conquering monsters I shall be going about!
After accomplishing this with monsters I shall be
  going about!

Pleasant again it has become.
Pleasant again it has become.
Pleasant again it has become.
Pleasant again it has become.
Pleasant again it has become.[16]

The Unraveling Rite. Medicine and pollen are applied to slip-knotted strings. Each is held to a certain part of the body of the one suffering while the knots are pulled out. These ritual procedures are accompanied by the singing of songs that describe a progression of unraveling, extracting, and dispersing the malevolence of the enemy ghost from the body of the one suffering. The final song describes this malevolence as being dispersed far away. The unraveling concludes with the singer (medicine person) blowing away the malevolence that he or she has ritually loosened and extracted in the unraveling. When the unraveling is finished, the body of the ailing one is given an application of the unraveling medicine, and pollen is also applied. This is done to songs that describe a state of health and blessing. They celebrate the association being formed between the sufferer and Changing Woman and Monster Slayer. From this association will come the sustaining power of life.

The Blackening Rite. This is the final rite that should be considered as part of the prayer act. At this time the sufferer has his body blackened by tallow into which has been worked charcoal made from selected plants. It is accompanied by the singing of thirty-four songs. The plant ingredients of the tallow are associated with the events of the killing of monsters, but the tallow itself forms a black shield on the body which is associated with the flint dress and armor of Monster Slayer. The tallow is also identified as a medication. In the blackening rite the suffering person is identified with Monster Slayer and his powers to slay monsters. He is dressed as Monster Slayer, a dress which will protect him. He is given medicine.

The Significance of the Prayer Act. We have at the surface of the prayer text the rather simple message which invokes a holy person and then seeks identification between the one praying and the powers of the holy person. This leads to a request for the holy person to remove and disperse the malevolence which is causing such suffering so that a state of health and happiness can be achieved. The language of the prayer could even be viewed as the description of this process taking place. However, much of the prayer act exceeds this relatively simple message. It is repeated a total of twelve times, not to mention the extensive redundancy of the message within each prayer. It is placed in the context of several rites which have corresponding associations. We must attempt to understand what all this surplus is about, what it means. On the hypothesis that prayers evoke a field of images and that they structure these images in such a way as to transform an individual's entire relationship with the world and even his or her own body, we must carefully analyze this field of evocation and associations and show how the prayer act creates and structures the images.

First, at the level of structure of the complex prayer set, we can observe that the first eight prayers invoke an association with four pairs of holy people who are well known by Navajos. This is accomplished in the first constituent of the texts. The constituent boundaries are indicated in the text by lines. Beginning with Monster Slayer and Born-for-Water, the monster-slaying twin sons of Changing Woman, there is a progression toward pairs who have less of a warrior image and more of a positive ordering capacity. Talking God and Calling God, the last pair, are principal figures in the initial acts of cosmic creation. They are even outspokenly opposed to war.

In the second constituent each of these eight holy people is identified as being at the place "waters flow together," the last place where Monster Slayer was seen on the earth's surface.

The next constituent of these eight prayers calls for and describes the identification of the whole body of the one praying with the bodies of each of the holy people named. The identification is described as achieving a state in which the person may enjoy pleasant conditions. The identification is parallel to several elements in the associated rites: the identification with Ripener and with Big Fly in the emetic rite, with the powers of the unraveling strings which are placed at the same points of the body, and with the black armor of Monster Slayer in the blackening rite.

In the Navajo perspective the act of identifying and associating a person with a holy person (*diyin dine'é*) is an act of creation or recreation. This is designated in this prayer constituent by indicating that the body form of the holy one addressed in prayer is "long life" (*są'ah naghái*) and "happiness" (*bik'eh hózhǫ́ǫ́*). These Navajo terms when conjoined are central to Navajo religion, designating a way of life that proceeds in a condition of health to old age, a life reflected in the world as an environment of beauty and pleasantness. This environment is attested in the concluding lines of this prayer passage. Long life and happiness are sometimes understood as being a male and female pair, the personifications of thought and speech, vital signs. They are the vitalizing principles. To be identified with them is synonymous with gaining life and existing in a world of beauty and pleasant conditions.

The prayer passage which follows describes the removal and dispersion of the foreign malevolence, succeeding upon the acquisition of the powers and weapons gained through the identification. The passage is notable in its reference to the malevolence as an object, a dart. The Navajo conceive of the life principle as an inner humanlike form that stands within all living things.[17] The dart is recognized as an intrusion upon this inner life form causing the illness. The opening phrase, "You shall take the death of the upright, of the extended bowstring out of me!" is ambiguous out of the context of the prayer act. This is a reference to the weapons and the staff of Monster Slayer which rendered death to the monsters. It refers to the situation of the warrior who, by inflicting death on his enemies in the fashion of Monster Slayer, risked attack by the ghost of the slain enemy. This passage asks for the removal of the effects of such attack. The verb sequencing of the passage is very important. It begins by referring to the removal of the malevolent object as a future event and progresses through verb forms to a conclusion which refers to the removal and dispersion in the past tense, as a fact accomplished. This language construction engenders a performative force which surpasses the description of such events and participates in effecting the desired conditions. In the following chapter I will discuss more fully the significance of this verb sequencing as a performative force.

The final prayer passage describes the state of blessing and pleasantness gained by the achievement of the removal and dispersion of the malevolence. The terms *long life* and *happiness* refer to the central concept of Navajo religion.

The progression of names invoked in the first eight prayers, from warriors to creators, is continued in prayers nine through twelve. While the constituency of these prayers remains unchanged from the others, these four are addressed to purely life-giving forces, the pairs White Corn Boy and Yellow Corn Girl, and Pollen Boy and Ripener Girl. The two prayer passages added at the conclusion rename Pollen Boy and Ripener Girl and drop all but the passages which petition these figures to put the inner life forms of the one praying back into "nice" condition, with the expected result of achieving a state of health, order, and blessing. These passages center on the internal parts of the person—the foodpipe, the heart, and the nerves—which can be restored because the ghosts or malevolent forces that were bothering them have now been dispersed far away.

There are a number of parallels in the structure of meaning among the various levels of the prayer act. These parallels clearly show that the significance of the message of the prayer is at one with the process of effecting the desires expressed by the message. The basic constituent structure of each prayer text is an identification between the one praying and a holy person, followed by the expulsion and dispersion of the malevolence, which results in and makes possible a restoration and the reacquisition of a state of health and happiness. Each of the twelve prayers in the set bears this basic semantic structure. But as the prayers succeed one another, there is a gradual change in emphasis, beginning with an identification with the powers of destruction of Monster Slayer and moving eventually to an identification with the powers of life and creation. While the passage which is concerned with the expulsion of malevolence is carried throughout all twelve major prayers, it is finally dropped completely in the two short prayers at the end where the entire concern is with the restoration of one's interior and the acquisition of blessing.

There is a parallel between the semantic structure of each of the first twelve prayers in the set and the semantic structure of the prayer set considered as a whole. Both move from an acquisition of the powers of destruction achieved by a process of identification, to the dispersion of the malevolent influences, making possible a restoration of the body to a state of health and blessing.

The parallel does not stop at this. The emetic rite has a similar semantic structure. The drinking of the emetic through the pollen figure of Big Fly achieves an identification with the forces that have the power to expel malevolence. The emetic is a medicine designed to expel the undesirable through vomiting. Even though the rite is noted by other interpreters for its powers of exorcism, there is much more to its meaning. The sufferer drinks the medicine with his hands and knees placed in physical contact with a pollen figure of Ripener. Both the substance and the form are strongly associated with fertility and creativity. This shows that in the emetic rite the actions and forms give expression to a balance that exists in the Navajo perspective between the acquisition of the powers of expulsion and death and the acquisition of the powers of life and blessing.

The parallel in semantic structure is also apparent in the series of songs that begin after the emetic and proceed through the unraveling. After the sufferer has vomited, the remaining medicine is applied to his or her body accompanied by songs which identify the various parts of Young Man at Jarring Mountain's body with the weapon-adorned body of Monster Slayer. This identification is parallel to the emphasis in the first few prayers in the set. The songs which Changing Woman heard on the return of her sons from killing the monsters are sung just before the recitation of the prayer. These are set in the aftermath of the utilization of the powers of death, and they affirm that the use of these powers is necessary to help put things back into their proper order. The unraveling takes place following the prayer, and the unraveling songs tell of the removal and dispersion of the malevolence. Thus, the songs sung from the emetic rite through the unraveling rite bear the same structure as the individual prayers and the whole prayer set.

At the conclusion of the unraveling, medicine and pollen are applied with the accompaniment of songs which emphasize the acquisition of life and creation. In these songs the major concern is with the achievement of long life and happiness—that is, with the means of life—and the minor theme is the relationship with Monster Slayer which makes this possible. This continues the semantic parallel with the prayer set, which ends with its emphasis on the acquisition of restoration and health.

The blackening rite which concludes this prayer act recapitulates the structure one final time. The tallow is associated with the acquisition of weapons, of a shield of protection, and of the medicines that can heal and restore life.

It can now be seen that the prayer act evokes a wide range of images, and in its performance it engages the sufferer in an intimate relationship with these images. All of the sufferer's senses are engaged in the prayer act. We can see that the significance and efficacy of this prayer act is drawn in the interplay between the double emphasis upon the acquisition of the powers of destruction and death and the acquisition of life and health. We may conclude from the analysis of the prayer act that the Navajo sees these forces as interdependent, but perhaps in ways that are otherwise inexplicable. The prayer act, according to our analysis of it, affirms that death may be essential to life; but it also responds to an underlying notion that to take upon oneself the powers of dealing death, as in acts of war, is to risk the potential danger that is associated with these rather awesome responsibilities. The danger is conceptualized as the malevolent intentions of the ghost of the one who has been killed. To deal with it requires the association and identification with the events told in story. In these stories each death caused by Monster Slayer was also an act of creation. Improper acts which cause death or mistreatment of the dead will likely cause illness.

The meaning and power of the prayer act can now be grasped in much greater detail. Death must not be inflicted on another except for creative purposes. When it is, as in times of war, ill consequences may result that are ascribed to the ghost of the dead. Enemyway and its prayer acts expel this ghost, but they may do so only by bringing the focus finally upon an act of creation. Until some creative act results from that death, the ghost can never be allayed. The significance of the performance of the prayer act is to evoke and structure the images associated with this situation in such a way that they create the power that can expel malevolent influences and that can reorder, and hence restore to health and happiness, a person who suffers.

Conclusion

The significance of prayer is extensively influenced by the associated ritual, story traditions, and pragmatic aspects of the prayer performance. These contextual spheres are heavily involved in the processes of evoking and structuring images and, in turn, are instrumental in bringing about the effects these images achieve in the world. Since a single prayer text may be uttered in a very wide range of contexts—one can even say theoretically an infinite range of contexts—it can be seen how a prayer act is not restricted in the influence it may have on the world or in the significance it may bear in its performance, no matter how formulaic it may appear. In this way then we may finally close the gap Tylor found to exist between the commonly accepted idea that prayer is spoken from the heart to the most specific of existential needs and the highly formulaic and rigidly structured character of prayer.

Epilogue

Having for some time worried about the nature of prayer and the pitfalls that seem to have accompanied the study of prayer, I have concluded that a set of simple distinctions would enhance the situation. The study of prayer must distinguish between prayer as text, as the words that comprise a prayer; prayer as act, the praying or utterance of a prayer within specific historical, cultural, personal, pragmatic, and performative contexts; and prayer as subject (what I call metaprayer), statements made within a religious tradition about the nature, character, efficacy, value, theology, and philosophy of prayer and praying. Not only must these distinctions be made, but the interrelationships among these aspects of prayer must be considered. Much is to be gained in understanding prayer according to each category, but much more is discerned when all three can be conjointly considered for specific prayer situations.[18]

NOTES

1. Dennis Tedlock, "Verbal Art," in *Handbook of North American Indians*, ed. William C. Sturtevant (Washington: Smithsonian Institution, in press.), vol. 1, chap. 50.

2. See, e.g., G. van der Leeuw, *Religion in Essence and Manifestation* (New York: Harper & Row, 1963), chap. 62, "The Word of Man: Magical Formula and Prayer."

3. See, e.g., R. R. Marett, *The Threshold of Religion*, 2nd ed. (London, 1914); Robert H. Lowie, *Primitive Religion* (New York: Liveright, 1970), pp. 321-29; and Paul Radin, *Primitive Religion*, (New York: Dover, 1957), pp. 185-91.

4. Edward B. Tylor, *Primitive Culture* (London: John Murray, 1873), 2:364.

5. *Primitive Culture*, 2:365-70.

6. *Primitive Culture*, 2:371.

7. *Primitive Culture*, 2:374.

8. See Sam D. Gill, *Sacred Words: A Study of Navajo Religion and Prayer* (Westport, CT: Greenwood Press, 1981), chap. 1 and Appendix A, for a critical discussion of Reichard's study of prayer.

9. Dennis Tedlock, "From Prayer to Reprimand," in *Language in Religious Practice*, ed. William J. Samarin (Rowley, MA: Newbury House, 1976), pp. 72-83.

10. Stanley J. Tambiah, "The Magical Power of Words," *Man*, n.s. 3 (1968): 177-208, and "Form and Meaning of Magical Acts: A Point of View," in *Modes of Thought*, ed. Robin Horton and Ruth Finnegan (London: Faber & Faber, 1973), pp. 199-229.

11. Philip L. Ravenhill, "Religious Utterances and the Theory of Speech Acts," in *Language in Religious Practice*, pp. 26-39.

12. See the following chapter, "Prayer as Person: The Performative Force in Navajo Prayer Acts." For further bibliography see note 1 in this article and Ravenhill, "Religious Utterances," pp. 38-39.

13. Gary H. Gossen, "Language as Ritual Substance," in *Language in Religious Practice*, pp. 40-62.

14. See Gill, *Sacred Words,* chaps. 1–3.

15. The principal source for the mythology and ritual of Enemyway is Berard Haile, *Origin Legend of the Navajo Enemy Way,* (New Haven: Yale University Publications in Anthropology 17, 1938).

16. Haile, *Enemy Way*, pp. 207-13.

17. See Gill, *Sacred Words*, chap. 4, for a fuller discussion of the concept of inner form.

18. For a fuller discussion see Sam D. Gill, "Prayer," *The Encyclopedia of Religion* (New York: Macmillan, 1986).

Prayer as Person:

The Performative Force in Navajo Prayer Acts

Doc White Singer, an old man knowledgeable in the traditions and ways of Navajo religion, told me about prayer. He said, "Prayer is not like you and me. It is like a holy person; it has a personality five times that of ours." I have heard other Navajos refer to the act of prayer variously as a person who knows everything, as a person who can take you on a journey down under the earth or up to the sky, and as a person who is all-powerful. The extent of the references to prayers as active agents, or more familiarly as persons, has led me to believe that this reflects the Navajo conception that prayer acts are active forces that can render effects on the world. In other words, the Navajo conception of prayer acts emphasizes their pragmatic character. In the recent philosophical vernacular of J. L. Austin, Navajos see their prayer acts as "performative utterances," that is, as groups of words the utterance of which is actually the doing of an action.[1]

Scholars have occasionally recognized that Navajos believe that their prayers affect the world, but their view of how that takes place has been to see prayer as magically compulsive. Gladys Reichard, in her *Navaho Prayer: The Compulsive Word,* analyzed the rhythmic substructure in Navajo prayers to demonstrate various repetitious patterns which, she argued, garner magical forces of compulsion.[2]

In this chapter I am going to exemplify a different approach by focusing on the structure of a prayer act commonly performed in Navajo ceremonials. I want to show that it is due to the structure of the prayer act, rather than to its magically compulsive character, that Navajos see it as an active agent in their world.

The uttering of the prayer plays an integral part in satisfying the needs which motivate the prayer utterance. From this point of view I

113

think we can more accurately understand the Navajo notion of prayer as a person capable of effective actions.

An Outline of Navajo Ceremonialism

I must preface my analysis with a brief outline of Navajo ceremonialism. The passing of seasons, the cycle of life, and the efforts to subsist seem to take a position in Navajo ceremonialism secondary to the exigencies of maintaining health. Most Navajo ceremonies are motivated by someone's illness. The acceptance of a persistent illness triggers a process bent on restoring health. First a diagnosis is made upon information collected by using techniques of divination to determine the cause of the illness. Normally there need be no physiological relationship between the cause and the symptoms felt. The diagnosis leads to a recommendation for a curing way and a specific ceremonial within that way. A figure called a singer maintains the traditional knowledge of the prayers, songs, and procedures of the various ceremonial ways. Singers normally specialize in only one or two of the many ceremonials because of the enormous task of learning the songs, prayers, and ritual procedures necessary to perform the ceremonial. A singer must be procured and arrangements made for the ceremonial performance, which may last from one to nine nights, including the intervening days. Singing is heard almost constantly throughout, yielding to prayers intoned at focal points in ritual acts. The variety and complexity of the rites which constitute the ceremonials reflect the richness and sophistication of Navajo religious thought.

Holyway Ceremonials

The prayer act which I have chosen for analysis is found in the context of a commonly used ritual way of curing known as Holyway. Holyway is used for illnesses whose cause is directly attributed to a holy person (*diyin dine'é*). Holy people are spiritual entities which Navajos identify with the power of creation and the life force of all things. The anger of the holy people is commonly traced to some trespass by the person suffering. Navajos say that the holy people place a spell (*áliíl*) upon or within the sufferer. The theory of curing calls for the removal of the spell and the restoration of the suffering person.

Many ceremonials may be performed within the general classification of Holyway, and each of these has an extensive associated
story tradition telling of the original performance of the ceremonial.
This kind of story features a heroic figure who journeys into forbidden places or performs forbidden acts. Predicaments of various
kinds, ranging from his illness to his complete annihilation, are the
consequences of these trespasses. Holy people are brought to aid the
hero in his predicament, healing and restoring him by performing a
ceremonial over him. The full ritual procedures, including prayers
and songs, are normally told in the story as archetypical for the
Navajo use of that ceremonial. The stories inform the meaning of
the ceremonial. Navajos maintain a close association between the
ceremonial and its stories. They identify the sick person with the
hero of the stories.

Holyway Prayer

The prayer act I have chosen is distinctive to Holyway. It is
intoned during the prayer stick and offering ceremony, which is
performed each morning of the first four days of all Holyway ceremonials. Prayer sticks are usually short hollow reeds that are prepared and decorated with particular holy people in mind. Offerings
of small bits of semiprecious stone of various colors are prepared.
Cycles of songs accompany the readying of these ritual materials
and their placement in cloth or cornhusk bundles. The subject in the
ceremony, referred to as the one-sung-over, is given these objects to
hold while he or she intones the prayer in litany fashion with the
singer.[3] At the conclusion of the prayer the singer takes the bundles
and ritually presses them several times to various parts of the one-
sung-over's body. Then, as songs are sung, an assistant takes the
bundles outside the ceremonial structure to deposit them in places
appropriate to the holy people.

The prayer from this ritual as performed in the Holyway ceremonial Navajo Windway is as follows:

Dark Wind youth chief, who runs along the top of the earth,

I have made an offering for you,
I have prepared a smoke for you!

This very day you must remake my feet for me,
This very day you must remake my legs for me,
This very day you must remake my body for me,
This very day you must remake my mind for me,
This very day you must remake my voice for me!

This very day you must take your spell out of me by which you are
  bothering me,
This very day you have removed your spell from me by which you were
  bothering me,
You have left to take it far away from me,
You have taken it far away from me.

This very day I shall recover,
This very day my body is cooling down,
This very day my pains are moving out of me!

With my body cooled off, I am walking about,
With my body light in weight, I am walking about,
With a feeling of ease I am walking about,
With nothing ailing me I am walking about,
Immune to every disease I am walking about,
With pleasant conditions at my front I am walking about,
With pleasant conditions at my rear I am walking about,
As one who is long life and happiness I am walking about,
Pleasant again it has become,
Pleasant again it has become![4]

This prayer is normally repeated several times, changing only the
name of the holy person and his attributes. This grouping constitutes a prayer set.

The prayer text can be divided into constituent parts to facilitate
analysis and discussion of the prayer act. First, the name of a holy
person is mentioned along with his distinctive attributes. Next, two
phrases mention the making of an offering and the preparation of a
smoke. Following this a passage beseeches the holy person to
remake the one praying, referring specifically to the feet, legs, body,
mind, and voice. Next is a passage which describes the removal and
dispersion of the inflicted spell. It is followed by the statement of the
consequent recovery taking place. The prayer concludes with a
description of an accomplished state of pleasantness.[5]

NAME MENTION

The names of the holy people, mentioned in the first prayer constituent, normally refer to those who are active characters in the corresponding ceremonial origin story. For example, Dark Wind, who is named in this Navajo Windway prayer, appears frequently in Navajo Windway stories. In one instance his help was sought to cure the hero, Older Brother, and his brother and two sisters when they ate a forbidden plant and became ill.

OFFERING/SMOKE

The second constituent, "I have made an offering for you, / I have prepared a smoke for you!" refers to the prayer stick and offering bundles. The hollow prayer stick reeds are cut in designated lengths and filled with tobacco. The open ends of the reeds are sealed with moistened pollen, and a rock crystal is held so that the enlivening light entering the smoke hole of the ceremonial hogan is directed to the tips of the prayer sticks. The prayer sticks are placed in cloth bundles containing fragments of turquoise, abalone, white shell, and jet as offerings.

The purpose for designating the prayer sticks and bundles as offering and smoke is illuminated by an event commonly recounted in ceremonial origin stories. In Holyway stories a sequence of episodes describes the procurement of the help of the holy person who is believed to be offended by the sufferer's trespass. This help is considered essential, for only the holy person can relieve the situation. An intermediary is sent to the holy person bearing a gift of one laced bundle. He presents this gift to the holy person with a ritual gesture, but the holy person makes no acknowledgment. The intermediary returns with two laced bundles, but the response is the same. After trying three and four such bundles, without success, those seeking his help conclude that they must be approaching the holy person incorrectly. They seek the help of someone who, they are told, knows the right address and gift. An episode is sometimes necessary to tell how this information is obtained, but eventually forthcoming is a description of the proper gift for the sought-after holy person and the design of the prayer stick which must accompany it. With these prepared, the intermediary returns to the holy person, who immediately acknowledges the gift and says to the messenger, "Go ahead then, my grandchild, prepare me a smoke." A cloth is laid down upon which the smoking elements are prepared. Tobacco is placed in the pipe and a rock crystal is held up to the sun so the sunlight may be directed to light the pipe. After the holy person smokes, the messenger is given the pipe to smoke. The holy person addresses the messenger, "All right, my grandchild, what can happen to him!" He knows the desires of the messenger without ever being asked. He continues, "I will positively return to my grandchild! What can happen to him? In four days I will follow you." But the messenger is unsatisfied with a four-day delay and implores the holy person to return with him immediately. Yielding, the holy person says, "All right, my grandchild, let us go then!" And they depart to perform the cure for the suffering hero.

The meaning of the words which name a holy person and announce that an offering and smoke have been made may be understood at various levels. In the limited context of the immediate ritual acts of the prayer stick rite they are simple descriptive statements which refer to the completed manual tasks of preparing the prayer sticks and the offering bundles. At this level of meaning the words perform in a locutionary sense, in Austin's vernacular, in that they refer to, or describe, an event which has taken place.[6] This is confirmed by the perfective mode of the Navajo verbs used to designate completed acts.[7] Recall the phrases, "I have made" (*'ishła*) and "I have prepared" (*nádįįlá*).

But when these constituents are seen in light of Navajo religious tradition as borne in story, another level of meaning is revealed. The words of these first two prayer constituents make reference not only to the manual acts which precede the prayer utterance but also to the events told in the stories which established the Holyway procedures for getting the help of a holy person. Here the words of the prayer, along with the ritual acts associated with the prayer sticks and offerings, constitute the proper procedures for acquiring this helper. The utterance of this part of the prayer in the appropriate ritual context amounts to the acts necessary to establish the kind of relationship with a holy person that obliges him to respond to certain requests made of him. It is the relationship of "grandfather" to "grandchild." It is the performance of the speech act as conventionalized in ceremony that seeks to establish a relationship, and thus it carries, in Austin's terms, an illocutionary force. The performance of this part of the act has a certain conventional force.

IMPERATIVE TO REMAKE

The next constituent of the prayer amounts to an imperative to remake: "This very day you must remake my feet for me," and so on. This passage confirms the performative effect of the preceding passage in that it assumes that the holy person is attentive and that a relationship is established in which the holy person may be addressed directly in an imperative verbal mode. It does not humbly ask a favor of the holy person; it beseeches the holy person to remake the feet, legs, body, mind, and voice of the sufferer.

The significance of the catalog of body parts is illuminated in Navajo creation stories. The Navajo conception of life is presented as a humanlike form (*bii'gistíín*) which stands within all living physical forms—mountains, rivers, plants, and animals. The placement of the humanlike inner life form within the outer physical form is the basic act of creation as revealed in the study of Navajo creation stories.[8] This act focuses on the correspondence of the inner and outer forms at these particular body parts. The correspondence is often expressed in ritual by the manual act of pressing at the body parts concerned, effecting life entering the physical form. Thus, the act of remaking in Holyway is an act of re-creation. It is enacted in Holyway ritual as the prayer stick and offering bundles are pressed to the body of the one-sung-over at these named places.

REMOVAL AND DISPERSION

The prayer constituent beseeching the holy person to act has a pragmatic effect in that the utterance of the words exerts a force upon the holy person addressed. The constituent bears an illocutionary force of an "exercitive type" in Austin's categorization. These exercitives are the exercising of power, rights, and/or influence.[9] Following the utterance of words which effect an obligatory relationship between the one praying and the holy person addressed, a response to the beseechment should be anticipated. According to the conventional response the holy person should fulfill his obligation by removing the spell and allowing the return of health. Austin reminded us that the exercitive force of beseechment invites, by convention, a response or sequel. And indeed the next constituent of the prayer describes the progressive removal and dispersion of the inflicted spell.

> This very day you must take your spell out of me by which you are bothering me,
> This very day you have removed your spell from me by which you were bothering me,
> You have left to take it far away from me,
> You have taken it far away from me.

The Navajo verbal modes of the constituent reveal a shift from the imperative—"you *must* take it out of me" (*shá'áádíídłííł*)—to the perfective mode—"you *have* taken it out of me" (*shąhanéinílá*) and "you *have* taken it away" (*dahnídinilá*). Beginning with an imperative, "You must take it out of me," the prayer constituent concludes in the perfective indicating the completion of the act of removal.

RECOVERY

The expected response to the imperative to remake is thus begun, but it is a partial one, for it only removes the bothersome object. The concluding constituents describe the recovery taking place.

> This very day I shall recover,
> This very day my body is cooling down,
> This very day my pains are moving out of me!

Again the verbal mode of this constituent is telling. The Navajo verb of the phrase "I shall recover" is in the iterative mode, indicating the repeated return to a state once held. The verb, *náádideshdááł*, would translate literally something like "I shall start right now to go again like I went before." It indicates that the action is beginning in the immediate present. The Navajo verb translated as "is cooling" (*hodínook'eeł*) is in the progressive mode, indicating that the action of cooling is taking place as the words are being uttered. Hence, the shift in verbal mode indicates that the act is initiated and is progressing as the prayer is being uttered.

PLEASANTNESS REGAINED

The prayer utterance closes with the repetition of the verb *naasháadoo*, rendered here as "I am walking about": "With my body cooled off, I am walking about, / With my body light in weight, I am walking about," and so on. *Naasháadoo* is a verb in the progressive mode, with a continuative aspect. In other words, the form of the verb indicates that the action is in progress and that it will continue or endure. The other verbs in this passage are in the perfective mode, indicating that the action has been completed.

This passage maintains the correspondence between the prayer and the episode in the ceremonial origin story. It presents in summary the curing of the hero and his recovery to a state of good health. The state of health is expressed in terms of coolness, lightness in weight, feeling of easiness, and a state of immunity to disease. These terms clearly refer to the physical state, but the state of health is also expressed as being surrounded by a pleasant environment, designated by the Navajo word *hózhǫ́ǫ*. This was the condition obtained at the completion of the process of creating life on the earth's surface. When the world had been created with all of its living features, two holy people were sent to the tops of the mountains to view the new creation. From these high vantage points they found a world which they described as *hózhǫ́ǫ*, "simply beautiful." Thus, through the prayer act the one-sung-over regains a condition of *hózhǫ́ǫ*, an environment fitting the pristine beauty of creation, in which he or she may walk about.

Finally, the words of the prayer identify the one-sung-over with long life and happiness. "As one who is long life and happiness I am walking about." In English the terms *long life* and *happiness* have an admirable enough character, but they are two of the most important terms in Navajo religious language—*sǫ'ah naghái bik'eh hózhǫ́ǫ*.[10] In creation stories these terms are personified as a young man and woman whose beauty was without equal. They were among the first of the forms to be created. They are described as the means by which life moves through time. They are the kinetic force of life. They are also identified with speech and thought, which are essential to the process of creation and the maintenance of life through time. Hence, from the perspective of Navajo religious traditions, the identity of the one-sung-over with long life and happiness is the ultimate expression of health regained.

The prayer concludes with the conventional phrase, "Pleasant again it has become," which is repeated twice for each prayer in the set and an additional two times after the concluding prayer.

The Prayer as a Pragmatic Act

The pragmatic effect of uttering the prayer must be realized in the context of the situation motivating the act. In this case it is a part of a ceremonial enacted to cure an individual who is sick. The one suffering the illness is the one who utters the prayer with the singer. At the surface level the prayer is uttered as a prayer of intercession by the singer and as a prayer of petition and beseechment by the one-sung-over. But on the basis of my analysis of the prayer as a ritual act in a religious tradition, other levels of meaning have been revealed. The structure of the prayer is identical to the effect the prayer seeks, the restoration of health. It mentions the name and distinctive attributes of the holy people who are thought to be responsible for the suffering. It reports that an offering and smoke have been prepared for the holy people, and it engages them in binding relationships of reciprocity. It beseeches these holy people to remake the sufferer, an act they are obliged to perform. The subsequent removal of the spell, its dispersion to a place far away, and the return to health are described by the prayer as they take place.

It is clear that the significance of the prayer is dependent not only on the situation that motivates its utterance but also on the intended pragmatic effect. But it must be observed that the physical symptoms of the sickness which motivate the act and their physiological causes are not the primary field intended to be affected by the prayer act. It is not directed toward physical symptoms or to their physiological causes but rather toward the establishment of relationships with spiritual entities, the holy people. The illness suffered is attributed to the impairment of spiritual relationships. The physical symptoms of illness are only the manifestation of this situation. Hence, at its core the prayer act is a religious act, yet it functions at one level as a medical act. In terms of Navajo thought the prayer act is significant as a religious act of communicating at a spiritual level. This is what is distinctive of any act of prayer. The effect of this religious act is thought to be reflected in the return of physical health. But it is impossible to perceive the pragmatic character of the prayer act as curative in a physical sense without first considering it as a religious act.

Much effort has been expended in the study of Navajo ceremonials from the perspective of Western scientific medical practice.[11] Theories of psychological techniques, of physical therapeutics, and folk phamacology have been advanced to demonstrate the pragmatic significance of the ceremonial practices. Where these are found to be inadequate, theories of magical control have been advanced. Still, these explanations seem partial and inadequate. They are burdened with a host of insoluble problems when held against the whole fabric of Navajo ceremonialism. In order to realize more fully the significance these prayer acts have for Navajo people, Navajo ceremonials must be considered as religious events in which Navajos participate in the meaningful way of life revealed to them by the holy people as told in stories set in a primordial era. The pragmatic effects of the prayer are directed toward the spiritual realm. But as the prayer text shows, there is an expected attendant change in the physical world.

The prayer act is therefore not simply a curing act, but a religious act of curing. When it is seen as a total integrated act, illuminated by the religious traditions, it becomes evident that it is meaningful to those who perform it not simply because it cures physical ailments, but because it performs the acts which institute and maintain a particular way of life. Its semantic structure is composed of a sequence of words and related actions significant in Navajo religious tradition for what they do as they are performed. In the context of a Holyway healing ceremonial the prayer act is significant in being among those things a Navajo does in response to certain culturally recognized needs. It is the performance of an act of curing as much as is the administration of an injection of drugs by a physician in the Western scientific medical tradition.

The ritual prayer act focuses on spiritual rather than physical conditions. Yet Navajos recognize a correspondence between the physical and the spiritual world in much the same way that a sign serves as the vehicle for an abstract referent. This is demonstrated in the prayer act analyzed. When the relationship with the holy person was reestablished and he removed the spell, the consequence was described in terms of a renewed state of physical health.

The entire prayer act, including the manual gestures and the speech utterance, operates as a performative and in the perlocutionary sense, in Austin's terms, because it attests to the generation of a force that causes something to be accomplished—generally, to bring about a change in the state of health of the one praying. We can state in simple terms the perlocution: by performing a sequence of several conventional acts which constitute the act of prayer, the one praying is cured of an illness suffered.

I have used Austin's classification of types of performative not as a guide to the analysis of the prayer act but rather as a way to state more clearly the pragmatic character of the prayer act. The prayer act has been seen as performative in all three of the types Austin describes—locutionary, illocutionary, and perlocutionary. It has also been shown that the type of performative is dependent upon the extent of the context allowed to inform the act. In its most limited ritual context the prayer act can be seen only as a performative of the locutionary type. The prayer utterance has a certain referential relationship to the manual acts performed. When considered as a religious act patterned upon an episode described in story, it is recognized as a performative of the illocutionary type. The prayer act beseeches a holy person to respond to a given situation. Finally, when seen as a religious act of curing the prayer act is recognized as a performative of the perlocutionary type. By performing the act the Holy Person is beseeched to act so that health is restored.

Doctrines of the Infelicities

But these acts do not always obtain the expected results. After the performance of a Navajo ceremonial motivated by the need for a physical cure, it is not uncommon that the expected physiological or psychological effect is not gained. The person often remains ill or dies. In Austin's discussion, he observed that there is nothing automatic about performatives since they are not mechanical acts. He demonstrated that the failure of such an act must be accounted for in terms of contexts and intentions rather than in terms of veracity. Austin presented six rules, all of which must be upheld for a performative to be effective. The rules amount to what he called a "doctrine of the infelicities," which demonstrates the important point that the performative is happy or unhappy as opposed to true or false.[12]

Navajos have not been silent on the occasions when ceremonials fail to cure. A systematic appraisal of the Navajo explanations given for failure would essentially amount to a Navajo doctrine of the infelicities. If formalized, it would include these rules:

1. The diagnosis must be correct and complete. If the diagnosis discerns the wrong cause, an inadequate ceremonial process will be used and, consequently, will be ineffective. Further, if multiple causes are only partially detected, only a partial cure will be effected.

2. The circumstances and location of the ceremonial performance must be appropriate. The ceremonial must take place in a properly consecrated enclosure. It must take place only during the appropriate seasons of the year. The participants, particularly the singer and the one-sung-over, must have proper and serious intentions. They must demonstrate these intentions by observing specific dietary and social restrictions before, during, and after the performance of the ceremonial.

3. The elements of the ritual process must be performed exactly as required by the conventions of the religious tradition as held in the memory of the singer performing the ceremonial. This requires that (a) prayers must be uttered word perfect; (b) ritual objects must be accurately prepared and properly used; (c) songs must be sung correctly and in proper sequence; and (d) the entire ritual process must be performed completely, accurately, orderly, and timely. Errors in any of these areas may result in the failure to cure.

The character of these restrictions has commonly been observed as consistent with the nature of magical acts, since exact repetition of formula and act is often considered distinctive of the character of a magical act. However, when the ritual process is seen as a sequence of performative acts, it becomes clear that the attention to accuracy is a matter of the proper execution of conventional acts. It will be recalled that in the archetypes described in story, the presentation of an inappropriate offering to a holy person effected no response and the hero continued to suffer. It is clear that careful and accurate performance of the prayer act is semantically necessary for the effect of the utterance of the prayer act to be felicitous.

Conclusion

In the above analysis I have shown that the act of prayer is a religious act of curing, and that when seen in this light the performance of the act has significant pragmatic effects. The way Navajos respond to ill health is not adequately understood when such central ritual elements as prayer are viewed as either magically compulsive acts or as pseudoscientific medical practices. For the Navajo health is synonymous with a state of new creation and sickness is a disruption of that state. In other words, sickness is a state of disorder. Navajo prayer acts serve to reestablish order by a process of remaking or re-creating. As an especially critical part of this process, Navajo prayer acts may be seen as a language of creation with a performative force.

I must emphasize that magic and mystery have not been removed from this religious curing process. They have been placed in the more appropriate sphere of the acts of the Navajo holy people, rather than being associated with the character of the performance of Navajo prayer acts.

The Navajo consider an act of prayer to be a person, indeed, a kind of holy person.[13] Upon the basis of the semantic analysis of prayer as a performative act, I believe that it is clear that this is far more than a pleasing metaphor. At the conclusion of the era of creation the holy people departed from the earth's surface to go to their own domain. Upon leaving they indicated that they would never again be seen as they were at that time. With this departure a great communications gap was created between the Navajo people and the holy people. The Navajo were left on the earth with the responsibility for maintaining the world as it had been created and the kind of life that had been revealed to them. They were given prayers, songs, and ceremonial ways as the means to do so. Bridging the gap between the earth people and the holy people is a crucial element in Navajo ceremonial practices. This is accomplished by uttering prayers who are thought of as messengers who have unique communication and travel abilities. It may be concluded that the very idea of the prayer act as a performative force is embedded in Navajo religious thought.

NOTES

1. Summaries of Austin's work (*How to Do Things with Words*, ed. J. O. Urmson and Marina Sbisa, 2d ed. [Cambridge: Harvard University

Press, 1975]) can be found in numerous works, including Ruth Finnegan, "How to Do Things with Words: Performative Utterances among the Limba of Sierra Leone," *Man*, n.s. 4 (1969):537-52; Stanley J. Tambiah, "Form and Meaning of Magical Acts: A Point of View," in *Modes of Thought*, ed. Robin Horton and Ruth Finnegan (London: Faber & Faber, 1973), pp. 199-229; and Benjamin Ray, "Performative Utterances in African Ritual," *History of Religions* 13 (1973): 16-35.

2. In my study of Navajo prayer, *Sacred Words: A Study of Navajo Religion and Prayer* (Westport, CT: Greenwood Press, 1981) I did not find a single challenge to Reichard's view of prayer as compulsive magic; see esp. pp. 191-98 for my critique of her approach.

3. I refrain from calling the subject of the healing ceremonials the "patient" and the performing specialist the "medicine man," as has often been the custom, because I feel that this indicates a predisposition toward an explanation based on medical ideology, thus precluding the perspective of religion. For photographs of a prayer stick rite see my *Songs of Life* (Leiden: E. J. Brill, 1979), Plates XVII-XXI.

4. This prayer text is taken from Leland C. Wyman, *The Windways of the Navajo* (Colorado Springs: Taylor Museum of Colorado Springs Fine Arts Center, 1962), pp. 182-83. I have made some changes in the translation based on a careful analysis of the mode and aspect of Navajo verbs. It resembles more closely the translation of the prayer in Wyman's *Beautyway, a Navaho Ceremonial* (New York: Pantheon, 1975), pp. 98-102. Both are texts recorded by Berard Haile. I wish to thank Clark Etsitty for his help in this translation task.

5. This is but one of eight major classes of prayer that I have identified and analyzed. See *Sacred Words*.

6. For a definitive discussion of Austin's classifications of performatives, see esp. lectures 8-10 in *How to Do Things with Words*.

7. The Navajo verb is capable of distinguishing as many as four different aspects and six different modes by alterations of the stem. The modes distinguished are: *imperfective*, indicating that the action is incomplete but is in the act of being accomplished or about to be done; *perfective*, indicating that the action is complete; *progressive*, indicating that the action is in progress; *iterative*, denoting repetition of the act; *usitative*, denoting habituality in performing the act; and *optative*, expressing potentiality and desire. The aspects are: *momentaneous*, action beginning and ending in an instant; *repetitive*, action repeated; *semelfactive*, action which occurs once and is neither continued nor repeated; and *continuative*, action which is continued. See Robert W. Young and William Morgan, *The Navajo Language* (Salt Lake City: Deseret Book Co., 1972), p. 42.

8. For the most extensive discussion of this concept see Berard Haile, "Soul Concepts of the Navaho," *Annali Lateranesi* 7 (1943): 59-94.

9. For Austin's discussion of five general classes of illocutionary forces, see lecture 12 in *How to Do Things with Words*.

10. For a thorough linguistic analysis of these terms, see Gary Witherspoon, *Language and Art in the Navajo Universe* (Ann Arbor, University of Michigan Press, 1977), chap. 1.

11. An approach dubbed by William James as "medical materialism" in *The Varieties of Religious Experience* (New York: Collier, 1962), p. 29.

12. In lecture 2 in *How to Do Things with Words* Austin states that the failure to satisfy any one of the following six conditions will result in the performative being infelicitous or unhappy: (A.1) There must exist an accepted conventional procedure having a certain conventional effect, that procedure to include the uttering of certain words by certain persons in certain circumstances, and further, (A.2) the particular persons and circumstances in a given case must be appropriate for the invocation of the particular procedure invoked. (B.1) The procedure must be executed by all participants both correctly and (B.2) completely. (C.1) Where, as often, the procedure is designed for use by persons having certain thoughts or feelings, or for the inauguration of certain consequential conduct on the part of any participant, then a person participating in and so invoking the procedure must in fact have those thoughts or feelings, and the participants must intend so to conduct themselves, and further (C.2) must actually so conduct themselves subsequently.

13. The fact that "person" for the Navajo is not restricted to human person is essential to an understanding of Navajo religion. For an especially illuminating discussion of the concept of person as it applies to the Ojibwa, see A. I. Hallowell, "Ojibwa Ontology, Behavior, and World View," in *Culture in History: Essays in Honor of Paul Radin*, ed. Stanley Diamond (New York: Columbia Univerisity Press, 1960), pp. 18-52.

Holy Book in Nonliterate Traditions

Toward the Reinvention of Religion

There is radical incongruity in the title "Holy Book in Nonliterate Traditions." A holy *book* is a volume of writings, and we might assume that it is to be read. Nonliterate peoples obviously neither read nor write. It therefore seems clear that nonliterate peoples can neither create nor use holy books.

Why then would I want to consider such a topic? Have I not in my opening sentences thoroughly exhausted the topic? The choice of title for this presentation is a self-conscious one, and its incongruity is intended not to stifle thought but to stimulate it. I avoided alternate titles like "Holy Book in Primal Societies" or "Myth as Scripture in Nonliterate Traditions." Such titles resolve too quickly the issues regarding the study of religion and the role of scripture in this study. We might consider the title "Holy Book in Nonliterate Traditions" something of a *koan*, but I assure you that what I have to say will proceed at only the most preliminary stages in the enlightenment process. Nonetheless I hope that by following it we will be led toward a reinvention of religion.

The Adversities of "The Book"

The original observation that, because of their mode of communication, nonliterate peoples cannot create or use holy books does not preclude that such people may be aware of literacy and books, that they may comprehend such a notion as writing, that they may evaluate writing and express clearly their views on it. When placed in the context of literacy, nonliterate peoples have often consciously chosen to maintain their exclusively oral mode of communication, and they expound the benefits of the oral mode

129

of communication over against what they see as the degradation and dangers of literacy. I am yet to be convinced that nonliteracy need be displaced with literacy, hence I caution against the use of the term preliterate.

The Zuni song, quoted in an earlier chapter, that remembered Frank Hamilton Cushing as the one who read his prayers while the Zuni said theirs from their hearts is evidence that the Zuni do not remember Cushing as some greatly superior figure because he had the power of literacy. Contrary to our expectations they seem to distinguish the very character of their religion by contrast with Cushing's dependence upon literacy. They see their religion as being of the heart, not of the head. They see their religion as performed and lived, not written and read.

We may find ourselves surprised that these people are making comparisons of themselves with us, that they are using us and writing, our emblem of civilization, to state their own superiority—and in a poetic form at that! The Zuni are the Native Americans of whom it was said less than a century ago that their language was so crude that they could not make themselves understood without extensive use of the hands. Thus, it was insightfully concluded that they could not communicate with one another in the dark. For me, there is a particular pleasure to find that they are looking at, evaluating, and imagining us as we are doing the same to them.

Such self-conscious distinctions are commonly made by nonliterate peoples the world over when confronted by literate peoples. This confrontation has invariably taken place in the situation of colonization and conquest. Thus, the responses of nonliterate peoples have been in the context of oppression and disruption. This situation has clearly shaped the character of the comments they have made. Nonliterate peoples in these situations have typically been confronted first by missionaries who have tried to teach them to read so that they might read scripture, then by governmental agencies who presented written documents as authority for their rights to the lands and possessions of the nonliterate peoples. They have been confronted by a whole system of economic exchange that is mediated by written orders, letters, and printed paper money. Then, when they ceased to be threatening or disruptive to colonial efforts, ethnologists, folklorists, and anthropologists have rushed in to study them before they lost their "primitive" characteristics or became extinct. These observers have taken *notes* and written *books* about the peoples they observe.

It is this background of oppression that frames many of the comparisons nonliterate peoples have made between themselves and the intruding outsiders. Here are some examples.

A member of the Carrier tribe in British Columbia compared his people's knowledge of animals to that of European-Americans. He said, "The white man writes everything down in a book so that it might not be forgotten; but our ancestors married the animals, learned their ways, and passed on the knowledge from one generation to another."[1] This Native American suggests that writing promotes forgetfulness and that the fullness of knowledge is gained through intimate experience and through face-to-face transmission. He voices the superiority of Native Americans over European-Americans on the basis of the natives' lack of writing. It is also notable that many peoples identify the unity of language, its mutual intelligibility among peoples, including animal peoples, as a designation of the primordial or paradisiacal era.

The Reverend Mr. Cram, a Boston missionary, visited the Seneca in the summer of 1805. In a formal setting he spoke to the Seneca in an attempt to persuade them to become Christians. After he spoke for some time, he invited the Seneca to discuss his remarks among themselves and give him a reply. Red Jacket was selected to respond on behalf of the Seneca. Among his remarks he made the following statements:

> *Brother*: Continue to listen.
> You say that you are sent to instruct us how to worship the Great Spirit agreeably to his mind, and, if we do not take hold of the religion which you white people teach, we shall be unhappy hereafter. You say that you are right and we are lost. How do we know that to be true? We understand that your religion is written in a book. If it was intended for us as well as you, why has not the Great Spirit given to us, and not only to us, but why did he not give to our forefathers, the knowledge of that book, with the means of understanding it rightly? We only know what you tell us about it. How shall we know when to believe, being so often deceived by the white people?

Brother: You say there is but one way to worship and serve the Great Spirit. If there is but one religion, why do you white people differ so much about it? Why not all agree, as you can all read the book?[2]

Red Jacket raised herein some profound issues: the nature of scripture as authority; the access to scripture and thus the access to truth being seemingly incidentally dependent upon literacy; and the issue of multiple and conflicting interpretations of scripture, especially as manifest in the observed actions of Christians.

In a similar vein an old Inuit woman whose name was Arnaluk told Danish ethnologist Knud Rasmussen:

Our forefathers talked much of the making of the world and of men—at that time so very long ago.

They did not understand how to hide words in strokes, like you do; they only told things by word of mouth, the people who lived before us; they told many things, and that is why we are not ignorant of these things, which we have heard repeated time after time, ever since we were children. Old women do not fling their words about without meaning, and we believe them. There are no lies with age.[3]

In the context of missionary contact, in a somewhat humorous yet biting comment, Vine Deloria, Jr., wrote in *Custer Died for Your Sins*:

One of the major problems of the Indian people is the missionary. It has been said of missionaries that when they arrived they had only the Book and we had the land; now we have the Book and they have the land. An old Indian once told me that when the missionaries arrived they fell on their knees and prayed. Then they got up, fell on the Indians, and preyed.[4]

There is an element of irony in the fact that the homophonic base for Deloria's humor exists in English, not in Native American languages, and has its clearest effect only when written.

Another example. In the latter half of the nineteenth century a Wanapum man named Smohalla lived in the Washington Territory. This was a period during which an enormous transformation of the area took place. The first missionaries had entered the area at the end of the first quarter of the nineteenth century. The first treaties opening the way to settlement did not take place until after mid-century, but by the end of the third quarter of the century virtually all Native Americans had been confined to reservations. Smohalla was one of the few unshakable holdouts. In several of his statements that were recorded and have survived, he spoke critically of his oppressors, but he also criticized his own people, who had given up their ways in an attempt to take up European-American ways. Notably, the token acquisition of Christianity and literacy is captured in the image of "the book Indian." Of such persons Smohalla said,

> Many Indians are trying to live like white men, but it will do them no good. They cut off their hair and wear white man's clothes, and some of them learn to sing out of a book. . . . No one has any respect for those book Indians. Even the white men like me better and treat me better than they do the book Indians.[5]

There are many other examples, such as the following one from Africa. Mamoudou Kouyate, a historian, poet, and storyteller or griot, of Mali in West Africa said,

> Other peoples use writing to record the past, but this invention has killed the faculty of memory among them. They do not feel the past anymore, for writing lacks the warmth of the human voice. With them everybody thinks he knows, whereas learning should be a secret. The prophets did not write and their words have been all the more vivid as a result. What paltry learning is that which is congealed in dumb books![6]

And finally I quote Russell Means, an Indian activist, who in a recent statement focused on writing as the distinguishing feature between Indian and white. His article begins:

> The only possible opening for a statement of this kind is that I detest writing. The process itself epitomizes the European concept of "legitimate" thinking: what is written has importance that is denied the spoken. My culture, the Lakota culture, has an oral tradition, so I ordinarily reject writing. It is one of the white world's ways of destroying the cultures of non-European peoples, the imposing of an abstraction over the spoken relationship of a people.
> So what you read here is not what I've written. It's what I've said and someone else has written down. I will allow this

because it seems the only way to communicate with the white world is through the dead, dry leaves of a book. I don't really care whether my words reach whites or not. They have already demonstrated through their history that they cannot hear, cannot see; they can only read.[7]

In Defense of Writing

Upon reflecting on these several statements, we can easily laud the tenacity of those noble savages who, like the Zuni, choose to reject our faculty of writing and our holy books. They are the few; and we know that in our generation, of all the generations of human existence, these few are the last of their kind, the last ones to forgo, in their noble ignorance, the pleasures of civilization. We can overlook the threat, the challenges of Smohalla's statement about pathetic Indians who try to become like us, to dress like us, and to take up our holy books. We cannot expect them to acquire the full measure of holy book traditions by merely learning to read. They are like children playing dress-up in our adult clothes. We can sympathize with Red Jacket for his observation of the divisions and degradations of some Christian communities. We can even chuckle at the humorous criticism Vine Deloria, Jr., thrusts at missionaries, and at his dependence on English and on writing for the bite of his humor. We identify the mission approach he refers to as one of the past or nearly past.

But our tolerance, our acceptance, becomes more difficult, the threat more caustic, in the words of the African bard and especially the Native American political activist. We find it difficult to accept quietly these statements without rejoinder. Let me focus particularly on the *written* words of Mr. Means and imagine how our response to him might go. It might include something like this:

Now wait just a minute, Mr. Means; you are imagining us entirely too superficially. What of the great works of literature that writing has made possible? What of the great thinkers, the ancient prophets, the poets, the rulers? It is quite clear you have read many of their works. We know and we can be enriched by them only because they wrote. What of writing as the great tool of creativity and learning? What of the power of communication that brings the world closer together, the power that even you, Mr. Means, acquire by letting your speech be written. I think that you care more than you say that we read your words. This written form of your hostile remarks will survive your voice, and even your flesh and bones.

Then too, Mr. Means, as we begin to think of it, even as peoples of the book, we are not limited to the written word. If you would only read the first words in the Genesis account of creation, and I suspect that you have, you would find that we do not believe that God *wrote*, but that he *said*, "Let there be light" and because of this act of speech, light came to be. And if you had studied the first words of the Gospel according to John you would know that our conception of "the Word" in the opening verse that says "In the beginning was the Word, and the Word was with God, and the Word was God" is rooted in the Greek *logos* and refers to God's creative action, a concept not unlike that so commonly espoused by your peoples.

And even one of our greatest teachers, the Greek philosopher Socrates, once said, "The discovery of the alphabet will create forgetfulness in the learners' souls, because they will not use their memories; they will trust to the external written characters and not remember of themselves.... You give your disciples not truth but only the semblance of truth; they will be hearers of many things and will have learned nothing; they will appear omniscient and will generally know nothing; they will be tiresome company, having the show of wisdom without the reality."[8]

Then too, Mr. Means, now that you have us thinking, when you consider even holy book people, in the many generations through which their traditions have existed, the great majority of these people have been illiterate; they didn't know how to read! Most of these book people couldn't read the scripture if they wanted to, and doubtless many of them never even had it read to them. While they have been affected by the impact of literacy on their world and their religious beliefs, they have maintained and practiced their religion through oral forms, through action, and through their way of life.

This personal level of the debate need be carried no further, but there are implications in it for the academic study of religion that I would like to pursue.

Implications for the Study of Religion

What features of exclusively oral traditions are being emphasized as positive in character? Let us listen again to the kinds of things that nonliterate peoples have said.

They emphasize the immediacy of their oral traditions—the immediacy of their religious experience. They stress the extent to which people must accept responsibility for tradition; that, in fact, their traditions, the accumulation of wisdom, the features of their cultures and ways of life are always on the critical endangered species list, for they are held exclusively in the minds of the living members. Religion, tradition, and culture must be transmitted face to face among the living members. What is forgotten is lost.

Still, to forget is not necessarily bad. I well remember trying to talk a Navajo elder into recording, with my assistance, his stories of creation. I believed them to be of a variety that differed from those that had been recorded. The old man became defensive and argumentative when I compared what he told me with what I knew were the views of other Navajos. I asked him if any Navajos were learning his wisdom. When he replied that there were none, I presented the argument that upon his death his wisdom would be forever lost—unless, of course, I wrote it in a book for him. His response required no time for reflection. He said, "If no one sees value in learning my stories, it is time for them to pass. If they are needed again, they will appear again."

What features of writing, of book-based traditions, are held forth as negative in character? Let us listen again to what these nonliterate peoples have suggested.

They note the tendency toward abstraction and depersonalization that may accompany writing. They point out that writing and reading may remove one from the immediacy of experience, particularly social experience. They point out that writing permits one the avoidance of responsibility, the false luxury of never having to learn, the possibility of detachment—all of which, from their point of view, amounts to a loss of meaning and a threat to existence.

While we are used to thinking of nonliteracy as a negative attribute, a sign of cultural deprivation, the very emblem of "the primitive," we may find ourselves surprised by these evaluations of nonliterate peoples and we doubtless find ourselves sympathetic to what they say. We cannot deny the importance of immediacy of experience and the acceptance of responsibility to participate in and perpetuate religious traditions. We can appreciate that a performed liturgy, a liturgy known and maintained through long and careful rehearsal and repetition, is often more emotive and engaging than a liturgy where keeping one's place in a stream of unfamiliar words on a page can become the overwhelming concern. We can appreciate the importance of accepting the responsibility for performing and transmitting religious traditions. We can appreciate the value of religion as it influences the many actions and orientations of human life, being inseparable from that very foundation that makes life meaningful. All these notions are inseparable from our ideas of what constitutes the religious dimension of human life.

What should we make of this rather frustrating experience of seeing ourselves reflected through the comments of nonliterate peoples? Can they be wholly in error? Have they no basis whatever for their comments? Perhaps it is just that their views of our world view and understanding of religion are biased because their contact has been made primarily with missionaries, governmental officials, entrepreneurs, and ethnologists whose use of writing can be linked with these potentially negative qualities. Still, we must ask if this kind of emphasis extends to our study of scripture, to our conceptions of the interrelationship of scripture to religion, and, even more broadly, to the modern academic study of religion. I believe we must conclude that it most certainly does. Thus, what nonliterate peoples have said may provide an insightful critical perspective on the academic study of religion, and in the light thus acquired we may see our way toward a reinvention of religion.

There are two dimensions that I would like to discuss. The *horizontal* dimension has to do with the accepted purview of the study of religion—that is, with the data and kind of data on which we conduct our study. The *vertical* dimension has to do with the interpretive approach or style of hermeneutic we tend to use in the study of religion. Both dimensions taken together constitute our operative definition of religion.

In any discussion of literate and nonliterate perspectives, writing seems to be a crucial factor. While our work, our religious heritage, our civilization depend upon writing, the critical perspective advanced by nonliterate peoples suggests that writing is not everything; that writing does not encompass all that we would wish to consider as religious; that writing may have certain detriments perhaps inseparable from its nature; and that the absence of writing (exclusive orality) may have assets that counter these detriments.

Even a cursory review of the understanding of religious traditions and the way they are studied confirms that we have a major imbalance toward written materials, and even then toward very select writings called scripture. Canonized scriptures exist in but a few religious traditions, and not surprisingly these traditions are especially important to our intellectual heritage. Our study of religion has been, and presently is, largely, almost exclusively, the study of sacred scriptures (texts); the history that led to their being written and established within religious institutions; and the history of their interpretation into doctrinal, theological, and cultural forms.

The academic study of religion has been extended to include the study of religions of the East and Middle East and to the missionization of Africa, the Americas, and Melanesia; but it has not considered to any significant extent the thousands of religious traditions of peoples who do not write. The study of these peoples has been relegated to social scientists.

This is not just an issue of the extent of acceptable data. It is not just that we have limited the study of religion to certain traditions and to certain segments within these traditions, but we have also placed severe limitations on the form of the data we consider in those traditions we study. Generally our data must be in the form of text or conjoined with text. We may see how our common categories are determined by text and writing even in the terms we give to them. For example, for such categories as verbal and nonverbal, literate and nonliterate, and even the categories of myth and ritual, the defining and conjunctive principle is that of text or literacy. We do not say action and nonaction. We do not say exclusively oral and partially oral or oral and written. When we say verbal and nonverbal, we usually mean text and action. When we distinguish myth and ritual, we make the distinction primarily on the basis of text versus act. We commonly ignore the fact that stories are often told in ritual environments in a ritually prescribed manner. We do not account for the implications of our usage of the term *myth*, by which we usually mean the written account of a story. We rarely include the oral dimensions and contexts of the story form or even acknowledge the fact that such stories are almost never written down by those for whom they are religiously meaningful. Likewise, our study of ritual is usually based on ritual texts.

Thus, even as we extend our concerns beyond text, beyond scripture, it is with text and literacy directing our thinking, and the data acquired through such extensions can never be more than peripheral. As peripheral they speak only to further illuminate our understanding of text, of the written dimension of religion.

While I would advocate the expansion of religion to include more than text, more than scripture and holy book, and to include the consideration of text in broader contexts, this is not the sole issue. As I have come to see it, this is not even the main issue.

Certainly we are not about to give up writing. We are not about to turn our attention away from written documents. We cannot deny the value, the importance, the vitality, of written modes of communication. The obvious foolishness of such positions should be clear to all. I believe that Mr. Means has his criticism partly misplaced. And I believe that our response to him, our defense of the creative power of writing, is fully justified.

Modes of communication, the differences between oral and written materials, must be taken into consideration in the study of religion and culture. Jack Goody has shown the ramifications of modes of communication on thought and culture in *The Domestication of the Savage Mind.* I have attempted to demonstrate this in *Beyond "the Primitive."* But the horizontal expansion of the academic study of religion—that is, the extension of the data we study—will not lead to much revision of the study of religion or to any significant expansion of our understanding of religion. This expansion must come from another direction. Let us now consider the vertical dimension.

As I consider more carefully the comments and statements in this chapter made by nonliterate peoples, I do not believe that it is actually writing that is at the core of their criticism. The concern is with certain dimensions of behavior and modes of thought that writing tends to facilitate and encourage. And these dimensions are linked to the critical, semantical, encoding aspect of language. Certainly the academic study of religion has, as an intellectual endeavor and as the extension of Western intellectuality, strongly emphasized this approach. We interpret texts to discern systems of thought and belief, propositional or historical contents, messages communicated. Put more generally, we seek the information in the text. We tend to emphasize code at the expense of behavior, message at the expense of effect, and text at the expense of the performance and usage contexts. Thus the products of our studies appear artificial, abstract, and rationally and intellectually complex. And they often are. And this, in itself, is not bad. The products of our studies seem removed and isolated from the subject we study. And they often are. And this, in itself, is not bad. But the shift to expand our contextual concerns, to expand our domain of data, will not revise this at all, for we will still extract messages and decode symbols in order to describe systems of thought and belief.[9]

What is needed is a complementary expansion in a vertical dimension as well. We must recognize that to decipher information from religious data, be it text or act, is not to exhaust the data. This information-bearing attribute of language is but one among many meaningful attributes of religious acts. Let us call this information-bearing attribute *the informative function*. To designate other attributes collectively without excluding the informative, I propose the term *performative function*. This is, of course, but one kind of designation, but it serves a notion that religion, as it is actualized, as it is lived, *does* something even if that is to *say* something. To extend our attentiveness and to revise our interpretive methods in these dimensions would constitute a true revision and expansion of the academic study of religion. Coincidentally it would distract our attention from the less productive distinctions that break on literacy and text.

This concern with the functions of religion may call up the fears of a narrow pragmatism or a logically faulted functionalism, but I'm not convinced these are valid reservations. Students of religion have expressed offense, and falsely so, at what we identify as the social scientific reduction of religion to social functions. Our concerns are with the *religious* functions of what we consider to be *religious* data. And these concerns complement and extend, rather than replace, current styles of academic study. To this point in the academic study of religion we have largely avoided any serious attempt to comprehend how religion is a creative vital force in the world of common peoples, although we generally espouse this as an attribute of religion.

A New Model

The discussion may be clarified by a diagram (Figure 1) illustrating the dimensions discussed above. The horizontal dimension is the data dimension. This is commonly divided on the distinction of text and nontext, or act. The vertical dimension is the interpretive dimension and is commonly divided on the distinction of what is said and what is done—that is, the informative versus the performative aspect. The combination of choices among these two dimensions defines religion as it is operative for the chooser.

While a major statement might be made reflecting the placement of various fields, schools of thought, and individual scholars in the sectors of this diagram, a brief general statement will place religious studies. As it tends to be centered on the study of scripture, thought,

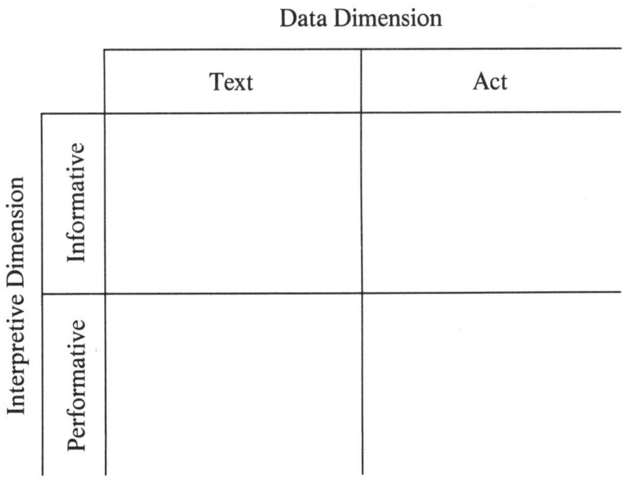

Data Dimension

	Text	Act
Informative		
Performative		

Interpretive Dimension

Figure 1

belief, institutional and doctrinal history, the academic study of religion has remained largely confined to the text-informative sector.

Religious studies has distinguished its domain from that of the social sciences, not on the basis of subject matter, for social scientists also study religion, but largely on the basis of the form of data considered—literate (scripture) versus nonliterate (primitive)—and more recently on the basis of interpretive method, eschewing the pragmatic, functionalist, structuralist, and systems approaches of social scientists.

There have been some leakages from and into this sector where text and scripture reign, but in terms of the major force of the study of religion these have been minor. Even the field that has been called the history of religions has not, with some notable exceptions, expanded significantly beyond this text-informative sector.[10]

Keying on the perspective gained from statements made by nonliterate peoples, I believe we have become highly constrained in our study of religion, and even in our study of scripture. I believe that we must expand in both dimensions to maintain and regenerate vitality in our study. What might be gained?

First, on the horizontal plane we must include in the study of religion all of the nonliterate peoples—those prior to the advent of writing and those whose languages are not written. We must include all of the illiterate peoples whose spoken languages have a written counterpart, but who themselves did and do not know how to read and write. We must include all of the folk—the peasant, the worker, and the common people. We must include, without the denigration usually assumed, those whose religions we call "popular." (Are the others, those on which we have focused, therefore "unpopular"?) We must include objects, acts, structures, and forms that we believe to be religious or that are engaged by peoples in religious action. In other words, we must destroy the data limitations that have made the study of religion to hinge upon literacy.

Second, the dimensions and character of our interests, our approaches, our interpretive methods must expand as we consider the broader performative functions of religion. This, as I see it, is the more important expansion. To make concrete the nature of this expansion let me begin by presenting a couple more examples from nonliterate peoples. These examples are selected to demonstrate the impact and importance of this vertical expansion on the study of scripture, the traditional center and core of our study of religion.

Along with the influx of Europeans into America the inevitable displacement and oppression suffered by Native Americans led to waves of prophetic movements. These took a variety of forms. A Delaware man named Neolin arose as a prophet in the eighteenth century. As did others, he presented a crucial message for his followers. He held that there was a way suitable for "the white people" and a way proper for "the Indians." While the white people could drink whiskey, Indians should not. While the white people could use guns and gunpowder, Indians should not. He proclaimed that Indians should abandon all "white" appurtenances. This Delaware prophet spoke his message to Indian audiences utilizing the metaphor of contrasting roads to heaven to illustrate the differences between Indians and whites. He used a map as a visual aid to his presentations. On it were drawn the respective Indian and white roads and the obstacles to be negotiated on the way to heaven. He said the map was revealed to him in a vision, and therefore it was not simply a visual aid; it was the proof and basis for his authority as a prophet. He called this map "the great Book or Writing." Notable also, the followers of the prophet were instructed to recite, morning and evening, a *written* prayer.[11]

Another relevant example occurred in a similar colonial situation experienced by the Papua in New Guinea early in this century. The example is from a cargo cult—as the millenarian movements in that area have come to be known—referred to as the Vailala Madness. The prophet, Evara, gave his people a message just the contrary of that pronounced by the Delaware prophet. Those Papua engaged in the movement were told to be disdainful of anything reminding them of their own culture and way of life. They adopted European-style clothing. They communicated with Jesus in visions. They called themselves "Jesus Christ men." They placed high value on European goods. And importantly, they began *reading* the Christian Bible. Though they were not literate, those people could be seen walking about, with Bible in hand, "reading" aloud. The book, as the European-style clothing they wore, was sign of the new life to come. "Reading" the Bible was instrumental to the arrival of cargo.[12]

Our first tendency, I believe, upon hearing these examples is to reflect with some humor upon the naïve ways of these "primitive peoples." But upon more thoughtful consideration we may discern something familiar in these examples. For the Delaware and the Papua, the book and the fact of writing are signs of authority, channels of revelation, transformation, and power. And it is clear that they do not believe this source of power depends upon or arises from some semantic or informational component of the words contained in the book or writing.

When we allow ourselves to be open to the possibility that "the book," the scripture, is religiously important as a religious object, not simply for what it says, we can recognize all kinds of examples where the Bible, as *book*, as *object*, is religiously important. Many are the preachers who preach and have preached with Bible in hand. The volumes they carry are tattered and worn, perhaps from being read and studied, but as likely from being carried and preached, from being presented as the basis for the authority of what the preacher says. This is precisely the use made of "the great Book or Writing" by the Delaware prophet. A considerable portion of the preachers that constitute the American Christian heritage have not been intellectually sophisticated and could likely grasp only elementary aspects of modern biblical scholarship. Nonetheless these preachers and their religious communities are in the mainstream of American religion. Another aspect of the religious importance of the scripture as object is to be seen in the common practice of owning and giving expensive and handsome editions of scripture. This often has religious merit, as in the giving of Torah scrolls to *shuls* or synagogues.

Even in a highly secularized and politicized era as the present one in America, it is upon the Bible that one swears an oath of honesty in a courtroom, even those who have never read a word of it or who expressly disavow the messages of its content and the authority it represents. The Bible is the book on which officials place their hands in taking oaths of office.

Beyond the book as object, as sign, the contents of holy books are commonly recited, chanted, and sung. In these performances the qualities of performance—sound, repetition, movement, objects, garments, gestures, and so on—are at least as significant and as effective as the informational messages contained in the words. Beyond this there are the many contexts where scripture is applied to life, where it provides guidance, inspiration, solace, and knowledge to meet exigencies and personal needs of all kinds. This is doubtless the most extensive use of scripture, and wherein it has had its most significant effects. We ignore these pragmatic and performative dimensions of scripture almost totally, apart from highly confined historical and ecclesiastical spheres—that is, apart from institutional and intellectual history.

What I am saying is that the holy book serves religiously in innumerable ways scarcely connected to any intellectual or historical significance of the words printed therein. The holy book serves as a cultural and religious sign, a form engaged in action and human behavior. I believe that for the majority of religious people the holy book serves more powerfully in these ways than in the informing of their intellectual and historical sensitivities.

In exemplifying the proposed expansion of the study of religion in a vertical dimension to include the pragmatic and performative aspects of religion in much wider cultural contexts, I have limited attention primarily to "the book," to the study of scriptures. Beyond "the book" there are many other forms of religious data that may be approached and interpreted when this vertical dimension is opened, such areas as liturgy, tale, prayer, song, architecture, art, tools and utensils, work activities, clothing, hairstyles, kinship structures, and language. All of these and many more are engaged in and by the religious life. They are the instruments by which life acquires meaning and value, and by which the world and all of its attributes are created and discovered.

NOTES

1. Diamond Jenness, "The Carrier Indians of the Bulkley River," *Bureau of American Ethnology* Bulletin No. 133 (Washington, 1943), p. 540.
2. First published in the pamphlet "Indian Speeches Delivered by Farmer's Brother and Red Jacket, Two Seneca Chiefs," prepared by James D. Bemis (Canandaigua, NY, 1809).
3. Knud Rasmussen, *The People of the Polar North: A Record* (London: Kegan Paul, Trench, Trubner & Co., 1908), pp. 99-100.

4. Vine Deloria, Jr., *Custer Died for Your Sins: An Indian Manifesto* (New York: Avon, 1969), p. 105.

5. E. L. Huggins, "Smohalla, the Prophet of Priest Rapids," *Overland Monthly* (San Francisco), 2d ser. 17, no. 98 (Jan.-June, 1891), pp. 212-13.

6. D. T. Niane, *Sundiata: An Epic of Old Mali* (London: Longmans, 1965), p. 41. My thanks to Philip M. Peek, "The Power of Words in African Verbal Arts," *Journal of American Folklore*, 94 (1981): 19-43, where I learned of this remarkable book.

7. Russell Means, "Fighting Words on the Future of the Earth," *Mother Jones*, Dec., 1980, p. 24.

8. As quoted in Peek, "The Power of Words," p. 43.

9. I have been considerably influenced by Michael Silverstein's lecture, "Metaforces of Power in Traditional Oratory," delivered at Yale and the University of Chicago, Spring, 1981. I want to thank Michael Silverstein for sending me a copy of the lecture.

10. I do not wish to imply that this expansion and redefinition is yet uncut or that I am in any way its designer. There are a number of scholars who are causing sector leakages. I think immediately of works in the areas of speech act theory, symbolic anthropology, semiotic studies, and ritual studies.

11. For further documentation of this prophetic era see A. F. C. Wallace, "New Religions Among the Delaware Indians, 1600–1900," *Southwest Journal of Anthropology* 12, no. 1 (1956): 1-21.

12. See Peter Worsley, *The Trumpet Shall Sound*, rev. ed. (New York: Schocken, 1968), pp. 75-90.

One, Two, Three:

The Interpretation of Religious Action

Some years ago, while studying Navajo prayer I spent a period of time seeking the wisdom of Navajo elders. Frustratingly, I found it difficult to get Navajos to recite prayers for me and my ever-ready tape recorder. In fact, most refused to say much of anything about prayer. While there are many stories to be told about my experiences, one in particular is appropriate here. On several occasions I visited a Navajo named Doc White Singer. He is a singer of ceremonials. Perhaps out of pity, but surely also with a wisdom that surpassed my understanding, he decided that more than I needed information about prayer, I needed a prayer said for me. Agreeing, believing that it would offer an opportunity to ask him some questions about prayer, I joyfully received his prayer and the related song he sang.

The prayer and song were from one of the Navajo Windways, complex ceremonial and story traditions, and like most Navajo prayers this one was complex and highly repetitive. I was attempting to do a structual study of prayer texts, so I wanted to focus on the significance of the patterns of repetition and change. After questions of a broad character about the prayer, I asked Doc White Singer about the order and the sequence of changes in the prayer. What I was trying to ask him, but in different words, was, "What is the significance of the order and structure of the prayer in terms of principles of religious belief and thought?" His answer was one that frustrated me at the time, and I have often pondered it. He said, "That's just the way we say it." And turning more directly to me, he held out his gnarled hand, and with a crooked finger he pointed to the digits of his open hand and, asked me, "When you count, why do you say, 'one, two, three'?" I had to admit that I hadn't spent

147

much time thinking about it, and I began to realize that my answer echoed the familiar Navajo answer to my questions.

I think that even if I were to have advanced some notion about counting being a number series, he would have asked why I call the first in the series by the name "one" and the second by the name "two." To these questions I would have had to answer with the same dreaded vagueness I had grown to expect from my questions to Navajos about their prayers, "That's just the way we do it," or "That's just the way I learned it." For a moment I shared some of the frustration I must have caused the Navajos with my persistent questions. I didn't seem to know how to answer such questions of significance and meaning. I could only think how unnecessary the questions seemed to me. I could defend the importance of counting by indicating the many uses to which I commonly put the number system. Thinking of my bank balance, I could certainly appreciate what horrors occur when one makes mistakes in reciting and applying the numbers. Of course, this reflected a question I frequently put to Navajos, "What if you mix up the way you say prayers?" To this question I always received a shocked look that seemed to say, "How could you even conceive of such a thing?" If the Navajos answered at all, they said that in such a case the prayer wouldn't work or that something terrible might happen. I had been bemused by these explanations, with twinklings of "primitive magic" in my mind's eye. Could that primitivity be in my mind? Usually the most Navajos would tell me was that the prayers were powerful when intoned and to say them, or to even talk much about them, without an existing need would not only be foolish, it might well be dangerous.

I was not totally discouraged in my thesis that centered on the meaningfulness of the structure of Navajo prayers, and I eventually wrote a detailed and somewhat technical description of the structure of Navajo prayer acts,[1] but in doing so I raised a number of questions about the way students of religion approach their work. Initially my approach was limited to the study of Navajo prayer texts, although I was well aware that these needed to be understood in light of the broader history, culture, language, and religious practices of the Navajo. I had no scripture or institutional doctrine upon which to base a general interpretation of Navajo prayer. But I certainly had lots of data, amounting to more than fifteen thousand lines (a measure that certainly makes no sense to Navajos, who are exclusively oral) of prayer text. I had an enormous body of story tradition. These stories recount the prototypical ceremonial performances, and they even include the prayers. I had information on the contemporary ceremonial use of the prayers. None of these data, however, had been written by Navajos. None is of the second-order nature of commentary and interpretation. And none carries authority for Navajos, at least as written documents, although the data reflect something of the authority of the tradition borne by the lineage of practitioners.

My initial view was that prayers existed as texts or as entities that bore messages—presumably between human beings and deities—and that the task of understanding the prayer texts was to understand the thought and belief system that lay behind their formulation and utterance. I was interested in the prayers as they reflected religious thought and belief. But when I asked about these things, Navajos referred not to what prayers mean or what concepts or doctrines they contain, but rather to what powers the prayers have when intoned in the proper setting. Indeed, they often spoke of the prayers as *persons*.[2] They spoke of what prayers do, rather than what beliefs and ideas they express. I was viewing prayers as largely transparent to some system of thought. I considered them of value primarily as they serve to reveal or communicate this system of thought and belief. In contrast, I found that Navajos were concerned more with the actions the prayers performed, and they held as irrelevant any attempt I made to formulate broad principles of thought and belief. To them this was demonstration of my misunderstanding of the power so evident in the acts of prayer.

I remember during one period longing to find the Navajo equivalent of the African Ndembu man called Muchona, who spent so many hours with the anthropologist Victor Turner discussing the significance and meaning of Ndembu culture and religion.[3] I wanted to find some Navajo who would tell me what it all means. But in retrospect I am glad that I did not find a Navajo Muchona, for that would have relieved me of the necessity of attempting to understand prayer and religion as the non-Muchona Navajos understand them, and I am certain that nearly all Navajos are non-Muchona Navajos.

Prayer is practiced commonly by Navajos, and to hold to the view that only a specially wise or intellectually inclined person—and one who especially enjoys conversations with outside inquirers—understands the meaning of prayer, belittles, in some fundamentally important way I think, the efficacy and value of prayer as practiced by those many people who hold that their lives depend on prayer.

What I was finally to comprehend was that the center of my initial emphasis, which was on the words of the prayers—on the texts—was not only inappropriate, it was simply impossible. Prayers are never texts, in the Navajo view; they are always acts that are performed for someone for some felt need. Thus when I asked about text, Navajos either refused to talk to me at all or they told me about the necessity of performance context before they could talk about prayer in any way. My concern was with text; theirs was with context and performance.

I found that I would not be able to understand the words of prayer in isolation from their use. I had to see them as acts in which many elements of Navajo religion and culture converge in a highly complex and creative interplay. Through complex analytical techniques I was able to describe an implicit structure of meaning that was unquestionably present throughout these prayer acts, but I was forced to consider a broader set of data on prayers and to try to interpret it in different terms than is usual for interpretations by students of religion. At the conclusion of my study I believed that I had made some advances in understanding Navajo prayer, and necessarily also Navajo culture and religion, but I was startled that the study of Navajo religion and prayer raised for me so many questions about the academic study of religion. In my frustrating efforts to study Navajo prayers I had to deal with the implications of the role written documents play in the academic study of religion. I had to struggle with the emphasis placed upon scripture and the writings of major figures and religious institutions. I had to struggle with the notion that whatever documents are accepted, the interest of the academic study of religion is largely in belief, thought, and history. I began to see that the way we study religion puts us in a peculiar position relative to Doc White Singer and to Navajo religion. There are no Navajo scriptures in the usual sense of canonized sacred writings, nor are there any second-order critical and interpretive written traditions of history, theology, philsophy, and doctrine. In fact, the person of knowledge in Navajo tradition holds that such activities, if even possible, are ordinarily to be discouraged. Such concerns are commonly understood by Navajos as evidence that one totally misunderstands the nature of Navajo religious traditions. I had to face the fact that when we take this approach of the academic study of religion, Doc White Singer and Navajo religion can scarcely exist.

It seemed to me initially that the difficulty I had in approaching the study of Navajo prayer and religion was fundamentally a problem of the character of the data. I thought it was because Navajos do not write that I had to make allowances. But considering this matter more fully, I now believe this is not the most fundamental issue. Rather it is our own interpretive emphases whatever the nature of the documents. The academic study of religion has usually interpreted whatever data it has had with an emphasis on text at the expense of context; on code at the expense of behavior; on meaning (in the sense of message) and proposition at the expense of use, relevance, and effect. We have looked primarily to the authoritative basis for religious practice rather than to the immediate effects and powers of the performance of religious acts. In a sense we have denied that religious actions are of value when we have considered them principally as an encoding of some underlying system of meaning. We tend to see value only in the underlying system of meaning.

I must stress that I understand this characterization of the academic study of religion as one of relative emphasis. It is not my purpose to denigrate the currently accepted approaches to the study of religion. Indeed, to discount these studies and to substitute an alternative would be inadequate, and is clearly impossible. In a very practical sense the academic study of religion has been largely a textual and historical kind of study because of the interests of the academic, cultural, and religious history in which it has existed, and in which the interpretation of scripture and philosophical writings in propositional and historical terms has been central.

In the face of the abducing experience of studying Native American religions, it has been of interest to me to attempt to develop and use an approach to the study of religion that would be directed toward the appreciation of religious action. This task has not been easy, nor completely successful. It has led me to academic areas I am ill equiped fully to comprehend, such as language philosophy, semiotics, and hermeneutics. This task has led me to reconsider our most common terms, such as *religion* and *symbolism*, and to attempt to restate the definitions and appropriate uses of these terms.

It has not been of much interest to me to present the approach I wish to advocate in theoretical or unapplied terms. Nor have I found it possible adequately to consider or present the intellectual history that should and does inform this approach. My interests in these areas have found focus on specific instances of the practice of religion; that is, my interest has been primarily in refining an approach in order to use that approach, not to describe it. Still, I recognize the usefulness of attempting some statement of the assumptions, elements, and biases of the approach I would advocate, however inadequate my statement turns out to be. The following is my attempt to provide this statement.

Religion

In recent years definitions of religion have been much discussed. It is commonly held that human beings are distinguished, in one respect, as religious beings. Forms and practices that we would commonly associate with religion can be documented as occurring in practically every human community. Yet, having said this, it is not so easy to state definitively what we mean by the word *religion*. Some hold to the view that since religion is concerned with the ineffable, the inexplicable, and the realm of spirits and deities, to define religion is impossible and the effort to do so is counter to its nature. I would hold that to define religion is to delimit the use of a common word and nothing more. A definition need not limit any essence or experience that is included in the category religion.

It is in our interests to use the term rather broadly. I hold that one aspect of religion is composed of those images and actions that to some person or persons both express and define the extent and character of the world, especially those images and actions that provide the framework in which humans find meaning and the terms of life's fulfillment. I hold that those actions and processes engaged in and used by human beings through which life is lived in order that it may be meaningful and purposive constitute another aspect of religion. Religion is the human assertion of power to shape and to create culture and history so that human life may acquire meaning, even beyond the limits of human existence. Yet while religion involves acts of creating the world and the meaning of life, it also involves acts and processes by which human beings discover limits and boundaries, that is, by which the shape of reality is discerned. Religion is then a distinct mode of creating, discovering, and communicating worlds of meaning.[4]

While religion is a creative and investigative mode of action, the student of religion must recognize that the religions of others can be known largely, if not solely, through what can be observed, often only through what remains as residues of these actions and processes. For the most part this consists of written evidence of religious belief, history, and practice, but it also includes numerous artifactual forms. It is reasonable to assume that these traces or imprints of religion are intelligible and thereby to conclude that they comprise a system of signs, a factor that has clearly influenced this definition of religion. The central task in the study of religion is shaped by the way these sign systems are collected, observed, ordered, and interpreted.

Humankind: User and Perceiver of Signs

The central theme of N. Scott Momaday's address entitled "The Man Made of Words" is illustrated in the Kiowa story of the arrowmaker. Momaday tells the story this way:

> If an arrow is made well, it will have tooth marks upon it. That is how you know. The Kiowas made fine arrows and straightened them in their teeth. Then they drew them to the bow to see that they were straight. Once there was a man and his wife. They were alone at night in their tipi. By the light of a fire the man was making arrows. After a while he caught sight of something. There was a small opening in the tipi where two hides had been sewn together. Someone was there on the outside, looking in. The man went on with his work, but he said to his wife, "Someone is standing outside. Do not be afraid. Let us talk easily, as of ordinary things." He took up an arrow and straightened it in his teeth: then, as it was right for him to do,

he drew it to the bow and took aim, first in this direction and then in that. And all the while he was talking, as if to his wife. But this is how he spoke: "I know that you are there on the outside, for I can feel your eyes upon me. If you are a Kiowa, you will understand what I am saying, and you will speak your name." But there was no answer, and the man went on in the same way, pointing the arrow all around. At last his aim fell upon the place where his enemy stood, and he let go of the string. The arrow went straight to the enemy's heart.[5]

Momaday shows us that the story illustrates something of the essential character of the imagination, and in particular that language is constitutive of being human. But the words by which the arrowmaker determined the identity—friend or foe—of his unannounced visitor are not so much an act to inform, to transmit information from one person to another, as an act by which the arrowmaker lives, by which he protects his life and the lives of his family.

Among the ways in which the human character may be defined, one emphasizes the possession of the distinctive power to create, to use, and to perceive signs. I include as signs not only natural language but also many nonspeech forms. And I include not only the use of signs to communicate information but the use of signs to effect results, to manipulate others and the world. In other words, for our purposes I would like to define humankind in one set of terms as a highly developed sign-producing, sign-perceiving, and sign-using animal. It is the sophistication and the distinctiveness of the use of signs that is the basis for this focal definition of being human. Furthermore, human beings exist in societies or cultures that share systems of signs—this being one of the principal lessons of the story of the arrowmaker. These sign systems at once define communities and provide the means by which their members may communicate among themselves and engage creatively in the life of the community. Now I must turn to a more detailed consideration of what is meant by the word *sign*.

THE SIGN FUNCTION

Since I have defined religion as necessarily involving the creation, use, and perception of signs, and humans as distinctive for their creation, perception, and use of signs, I must now consider the term *sign*. The term *sign* is a short form of the more descriptive term *sign function*. These terms will be used synonymously. The following discussion of signs is derived from the theory of signs articulated by Charles Sanders Peirce.[6]

We commonly use terms like *sign* and *symbol* to designate objects, things perceptible; but strictly speaking it is much more accurate to understand *sign* as referring to a relationship. This is why the term *sign function* is more accurate, for it directs our attention to a function, a relationship, rather than to a class of things, an object classification. First, and most importantly, then, signs are relationships, not objects.

A sign is a conjoint relationship between signal and sense; that is, a relationship between some form, image, or other delimited entity and a sense, meaning, or value. Both signal and sense are essential to the sign, for no conjoint relationship may occur without both. Since signs are relationships, we must understand that they are made only in the human mind. Indeed, many sign processes occur entirely in the mind, such as in thought. But the sign function may and commonly does begin or terminate with an external and perceptible manifestation or "imprint" of the signal portion of the sign relationship. Since signs that are wholly internal are unknown to observers unless expressed through signs that have an external dimension, our concern will be limited mainly to this subclass of signs. In other words, I will be concerned principally with signs that are relationships in which an external and perceptible signal is conjoined with an internal sense or value. The external dimension may be thought of as a vehicle or a sign vehicle, for it serves to carry the sense or value from the mind into the world or from the world into the mind.

To this point a sign has been seen as a conjoint relationship between a signal and a sense. But there is more. It is important to reiterate that signs are relationships and not classes of objects. They are relationships formed in the mind; they do not occur in nature, nor do they form of themselves. Any object in nature, indeed anything that is perceptible, may serve as signal in the sign function, but only if some mind conjoins it with sense. It follows that the same signal may be conjoined to radically differing senses by different minds at the same moment, or by the same mind at different moments. The appreciation of this elementary property of signs reveals the great error of misunderstanding signs as simply a class of objects.

Another aspect of the sign function must now be considered. I have persistently designated human beings as both users and perceivers of signs. This dual designation has been made to reflect the awareness that as signs are conjoint relationships, they are relationships formed to serve a purpose. The relationship may involve the creation and manifestation of a signal by the person whose mind forms the relationship. In this case the relationship produces not solely a mental signal, but a replica of that signal is also created which is perceptible external to the mind of the sign producer. I see no need to distinguish between internal mental signal and the production of an external replica of this vehicle since we are confining ourselves largely to this subclass of signs. The sign function may terminate in the production of a signal, or it may be stimulated by the perception of a signal that the mind conjoins with sense. In either case the sign function has a direction and therefore serves some larger purpose or process.[7] *Purpose* then becomes the third constitutive element of the sign function. The purpose or intent of the sign function is the way we may understand the direction and character of the sign relationship and its connection with the actual world in which it occurs.

Sign (sign function) may now be defined as a purposeful conjoint relationship formed in the mind between signal and sense. The subclass of signs we will consider are those whose signal is perceptible.

SIGN GALAXY

Given this definition of sign, it is clear that signs are significant and effective to the individual in whose mind the sign functional relationship is formed and who creates and uses signs as actions upon the world. It is just as clear that signs, especially the subclass we are primarily interested in, are also social. Speaking generally, for signs to be effective and to achieve the purpose toward which they are created and enacted, they must be supported by some system that defines potential signals and rules of sign use. This system must be held in common by a community of sign users and perceivers. There are no alternatives. I will call this assemblage of potential signs a *sign galaxy*.

In one respect a sign galaxy is the repository or reservoir that retains the tradition, the heritage, the experience, the history of the community that is defined by the sign system its members hold in common. All signs are intelligible and effective only in the terms of sign galaxy. Yet there is a complementary dimension, for all signs, as purposeful actions, are themselves contributing to the formation of sign galaxy and thereby to changing the sign galaxy in whose domain they occur.

Sign galaxies are composed of all of the signals (sign imprints) a community uses and the rules of use associated with them. These rules of use define the arrangement of signals in strings and arrays and the ways in which they are intended to engage the world. At some levels sign galaxies cohere around broad principles. Such central principles designate ethos and world sense, and they are commonly articulated in many disparate acts and processes.[8]

Signs and sign galaxies are then interdependent, but their natures are very different. The ways in which they differ as well as how they are interdependent may be shown by contrasting their distinguishing traits.[9] The distinction between signs and sign galaxies can be made in the terms specifically appropriate to our immediate concern. Religious action as it is observed is composed of signs, while religious ethos, world sense, and traditions are equivalent to religious sign galaxy; thus religious acts are distinct from religious sign galaxies.

Religious acts are always realized temporally in some present. They engage particular subjects, actual persons, as performers or observers of the acts. Religious sign galaxies, even if expressed or recorded in some form, are digested experiences, taking the form of paradigms, models, potential signs, and rules of use. They are the reservoir for the sign elements that can be drawn upon for religous action and the rules focusing and ordering these elements, but as sign galaxies they are always virtual and outside of time. They have potential, but no actual, subjects.

A religious sign galaxy constitutes a proposed world that is wholly contained within the system that is the sign galaxy. Only in action (only through the sign functions that constitute religious action) is the correspondence between this proposed world and the sensed world actualized. Through action alone is the world engaged, are persons actual, are effects achieved, does religion occur.

There is a remarkable correspondence between the resources that have been used in the academic study of religion and the traits of sign galaxy. Sacred scriptures, institutional histories, doctrinal statements, and philosophical and theological writings are not considered as religious action but as formative, paradigmatic, or normative elements in the description of some entity scholars propose as a religion. Each religion is, in a sense, invented in the terms of the documents and data that are considered; but because the entity proposed as a religion is contained within these documents, it is never actualized except through religious action. Certainly the processes of reading, digesting, interpreting, and writing that go into the study of religion are themselves actions, and perhaps even religious actions, for they take place in a present, they involve actual persons and actual worlds; but the product, usually a written document, becomes by its nature virtual, outside of time, and it does not have the capacity in itself to engage the world. Written documents align in character with sign galaxy, whereas action aligns with the character of sign (as act). Religion as action is elusive, since the mere recording of action, the setting down of a description of religious action, transforms it from sign function to the domain of sign galaxy. It eliminates all but the traces of the actual connection of the act with the world. Yet for religious persons religion is actual; it exists through actions; it engages specific persons, places, and things; it serves felt needs.

A Theory of Interpreting Religious Action

With this discussion of religion, signs, and sign galaxies as background, the outline and elements of a theory of interpreting religious action can be presented. There are a number of factors to be considered.

Understanding and Interpretation. Interpretation seems like a difficult and complicated procedure that involves the manipulation of the subject of interest. It suggests, by its nature, a violation and reduction of the subject. Why is there a need to interpret? Perhaps a simple familiarity with a religious action is sufficient to understand it. In theories of interpretation a distinction has commonly been made between understanding and interpretation. Understanding has referred to that effort to recognize what some subject means or intends, and that understanding may be derived in any manner, including attempting to put ourselves in the position of our subject, physically and psychologically. Interpretation has implied something more limited and controlled. It has been viewed as limited to the exegesis, or critical exposition, of written documents of all sorts and other more or less permanent forms, such as artifacts.

As it will be seen, while understanding is limited, it is important to the degree it focuses upon specific, or at least potential, individuals performing and/or observing specific religious acts, with the concern being to comprehend or to understand the acts they perform as intelligible from their particular point of view. The nature of sign functions, being conjoint relationships formed in the mind, necessitates that, in part, signs must be seen as being formed in someone's mind; actions, which are composed of signs, must be approached with the intent of comprehending them from the point of view of a chosen subject.

But, as has been noted, religious action is elusive and largely unavailable except as it is affixed in writing and artifacts. Since these provide the data, and usually the only data, ordinarily available for study, and since they are not identical with the subject of our study but only provide a record or trace of that subject, interpretation is therefore necessary. It is quite simply unavoidable. The stigma commonly attached to interpretation must be firmly absolved. Interpretation is what students of culture and religion do for a living.

While understanding as an approach to the study of religion is not possible free from interpretation and cannot be adequately validated, I would nonetheless not want to denigrate the value of experience, intuition, insight, and imagination employed by students of religion. As I will show, these factors are very important in the process of studying religion, yet not adequate in and of themselves.

Religious Action and Religious Sign Galaxy. Seeing that interpretation must be involved in understanding and in some ways surpass it, what is it that we interpret? The character of religious action and religious sign galaxy has been distinguished in rather radical terms. The interpretation of religious action has been encouraged, but action is elusive. Ordinarily we have only traces, remains, residues, and records of religious action. And these data are what constitute sign galaxy. Thus, are we to interpret religious action or sign galaxy? There is an interdependence between action and sign galaxy, and one cannot be dealt with without the other. An action out of context is impossible to interpret or understand. Sign galaxies cannot come into existence without a history of shared experience and action. While the religious actions of others may be observed and even participated in, the data, the evidence, subject to interpretation are not the actions themselves but some record or trace of the actions; therefore they are some aspect of sign galaxy. The recovery of the actions, and particularly the recovery of the qualities of action, must be accomplished in the process of interpreting the data we have available. This dimension of the theory of interpretation is central.

Meaning and Purpose. Dealing further with this interdependence of sign and sign galaxy may provide clarity in a discussion of meaning. We commonly ask the meaning of religion, especially religious objects and actions. Yet our common view of meaning may be misleading, for we often limit meaning to its semantical or referential sense. In other words, we tend to approach religious meaning by first designating objects and actions as symbolic, assuming that they encode some hidden or unarticulated meaning. Symbol and meaning are usually seen to be interrelated as a code, and it is then our purpose to decipher the code to discover the meaning. Many a symbol catalog and decoding guide have been prepared. Such an approach fails, I believe, on several grounds. It largely eliminates the creative role of sign users, beyond perhaps the selection of codes or the content of the encoded message. It largely restricts the function of signs to bearing messages. It devalues the signal portion of the sign relationship, for the signal is identified as transparent to the meaning. This is betrayed in the persistent asking of a religious action or object, "What does it mean?"

The theory of signs that I am proposing requires that to designate a sign is to articulate a relationship; it is not simply to set forth an object. And further, that to comprehend the sign requires not only an articulation of the sign elements conjointly related, but also the articulation of the character and dynamics of that relationship, what has been described as purpose. The matter of meaning and the burdensome issue of the meaning of meaning should not be dispensed with lightly. But in the proposed view of sign functions, there must be as much concern with purpose and effect as with meaning in the referential-semantical sense.

Meaning may be understood as an articulation of the sense conjoined with signal for a given person in a given usage, or it may be the articulation of the sense that is conventionally (i.e., within a sign galaxy) conjoined with signal. In a strict sense purpose cannot be a concern beyond a particular religious action, while referential-semantical meaning need not have this restriction.

Fixation and Reactivation. The study of religious action is commonly limited to a set of documents and records that attest to the existence of religion and religious action. One interpretive approach eliminates any of the attributes of action and behavior that have persisted into these records, thus autonomizing the action, and then considering the action in its virtuality as part of sign galaxy. An alternative interpretive approach is sensitive to traces of the attributes of action and behavior and attempts as a stage in interpretation to reactivate the data, that is, to discern how the data attest to action.[10] Reactivation requires the careful identification of the specific elements (signals) that comprise the event (the interrelationships of these elements in temporal and spatial domains, the actors and observers) and the description of the broader cultural, social, economic, political, and historical environment in which the event occurred. But beyond this delineation and description of the event in its context, there must be a sensitivity to the action character. Focus must be on those signs or attributes of signs whose specific function it is to actualize—that is, to engage the world, to engage other persons, objects, and entities in the performance of the actions. I tend to consider the action as primarily social rather than psychological, although there is no reason that a psychological interpretation need be excluded.

Informative and Performative. A distinction of the functions of signs is clarifying and useful. This distinction is not a classification of signs or sign events, but rather an analytic distinction made to help clarify the pragmatic or purposeful character of signs and sign events. All signs, in some manner, function to inform. They inform the senses, or they inform the brain or some other part of the nervous system. In one form this aspect of signs serves intellection and communication. We have tended to understand signs as limited to this informative function. Consequently we have confined ourselves largely to natural languages and to an equation of meaning with a semantical-referential sense. But this is only one aspect of the pragmatic character of signs. The other aspect or way that signs may be understood is that signs occur to perform—that is, to affect others, to manipulate the world, to create results. Indeed, even the aspect of signs that informs is but a type of performative function. Furthermore, the purpose of informing in the ordinary sense of bearing a message is rarely free of secondary purposes such as to persuade, to convince, or to direct. Thus, the informative and performative functions of an act, as the meaning and purpose of an act, may overlap or be interrelated, but not always.

When asking the "meaning" of a sign or sign event that principally performs an act to change the world, if meaning is equated with a semantical-referential sense, comprehension and intelligibility are nearly impossible. The study of religion has commonly put itself in just this position. By placing such an emphasis on this understanding of meaning, the academic study of religion has had no choice but to focus on philological and historical methods. And while there is no debate whatsoever about the importance and necessity of philological and historical approaches, perhaps even their analytical primacy, it is just as clear that they largely exclude and thereby diminish the importance of religion as it is practiced by the great body of religious persons for whom religion is a way of life; a way of creating, discovering, and communicating worlds of meaning largely through ordinary and common actions and behavior.

Recall the experience I had with Navajo elders. When I asked them what prayers mean, or about the significance of prayers, I was trying to understand prayer as primarily informative, that is, as message, a semantical-referential sense. Navajo prayers can be considered as informative, for they are composed largely of ordinary language, their manner of articulation informs the senses in many ways that can be described, and there is a propositional significance discernible. But the response I received from Navajos indicates that they understand prayers primarily as performative, for they invariably told me not what messages prayers carry, but what prayers do: what powers prayers have when intoned, what effect they have, what situations call for their recitation. And furthermore, the prayers themselves are elaborately repetitive and surpass all reasonable allowances for inefficiency and redundancy of message. Neither mode, informative or performative, is alone adequate in the interpretation of Navajo religion and prayer.

Stemming from the linguistic philosophy of J. L. Austin, particularly his book *How to Do Things with Words*, a focus on performance has received its most dramatic development related to speech, blossoming into a body of speech act theory.[11] This development has made important contributions to the study of religion and has demonstrated the importance of considering speech events as more than the communication of messages. What remains to be done is to extend this development beyond speech acts to the broad and complex domain of religious acts that includes speech and nonspeech forms.

Relevance and Importance. When focusing on religious action, intelligibility centers on purpose, on pragmatic concerns, and indeed on relevance. Action must make sense relative to the performers and to the situation in which the action transpires. Intelligibility is in this frame primarily a matter of relevance.

But once performed, an action contributes to a sign galaxy—to the formation of tradition and history—and in this frame of interpretation the relevance of the event to its performers and observers is commonly an inadequate measure of its significance in the larger social and historical frame. The meaning of action when considered in this larger frame may be described as its importance. The shift from relevance to importance correlates with the shift from religious action to sign galaxy, from purpose to semantical-referential meaning.

The Particular and the Universal. There is a common division in the styles and interests of students of religion. One tendency is toward studying the particular to gain precision and control. This approach is usually engaged in philological and historical specializations working with limited kinds of documents in highly developed and refined interpretations. The contrasting style tends toward the global and universal. This approach encourages multilinguality and the maintenance of interest in several, perhaps many, traditions and cultures, yet with some necessary sacrifice to philological competence and to the control of data and interpretive techniques. This kind of approach is interested in discerning and describing broad patterns, forms, and structures that occur among religions, or can be proposed as attributes of religion as a common dimension of being human. The techniques used are broadly comparative.

The one style or tendency is concerned with the study of a particular religion and even a narrowly defined subarea within a religious tradition. The other style is concerned with the study of religion or some aspect of it; religion as an aspect of being human.

To approach the study of religion so as to include religious action need not be incompatible with either style, for in the more narrowly focused approach, to consider religious action is to discern yet another level of specificity within a religious tradition. The broader approach may engage aspects of religious action—its form, nature, and character—as general comparative religious categories.

There is an interdependence between these approaches, for neither can be maintained in the pure sense, just as induction and deduction are finally not independent forms of logical inference.

An Aside: A Sign Is Not a Symbol. Some may have wondered why I have insisted on using the word *sign* rather than the more common word *symbol*. Several other items relative to the theory of interpreting religious action may be considered through a discussion of this distinction.

I have become concerned about using the word symbol because of the confusion of its uses. When applied to something religious, it may refer to a gamut of notions from a code system to something vague and unknowable but somehow meaningful. As a code, a symbol "stands for" or "symbolizes" something else. Here, as discussed above, the objective seems to be to get to the hidden value, to the underlying message, to the "symbolized." Because of the implied one-to-one correspondence of symbolized and symbol, and because of the placement of the meaning almost totally with the "symbolized" at the expense of the "symbol," I find this end of the symbol gamut of little value. While this view is commonly enriched and qualified in a variety of ways, its core is reflected in our common phrase "It's just symbolic," implying that symbol presents only an appearance and is not itself real. Sometimes this view even suggests that the symbol belies the actual.

The other end of this spectrum of usages presents a view that symbol defies understanding altogether. If symbol designates something unknowable yet somehow meaningful, there is not much we can do with it anyway. This usage often designates nonverbal signals in religion which appear potent but which we, being outside the event, cannot understand by means of deciphering codes or comprehending messages. To such observations we often apply the descriptive remark "highly symbolic." Perhaps what we have meant is that we observe the effectiveness of the religious act, and thus want to understand it as meaningful to its users/perceivers, but that it appears to us to carry no obvious message. Thus, we advance this theory of symbolism in order to include such events. When we say something religious is "highly symbolic," it seems to me that we index our sense of its relevance to others as well as our own confoundment in fully comprehending the terms of its importance to them.

Between these views of symbols are many others. Perhaps most common is the observation that symbols are multivalent, or polysemic (meaning that they have multiple meanings). From the approach I am taking here multiplicity of reference and meaning may be seen as a very important attribute when considering sign galaxies, but to insist that a sign (and we mean sign in the strict sense) is multivalent is questionable. Certainly a sign may be complex in its composition. A signal may be related to multiple, even opposing, senses at once, but this is not the same thing as being multisemantic. For when a sign engages relationships between signal and sense in this complex fashion, it is for a purpose—to form a pun or double entendre, for example. If the multiplicity is an unresolvable character of the nature of signs, then both user and perceiver would forever be swimming in seas of ambiguity. Even ambiguity, which is often a character of the sense of a sign, can be used with purpose and intent. If ambiguity is not intentional and perceived as such, it is simply a failure to conjoin signal and sense, and that is no sign at all.

Because it has been used in so many ways, because it has not been clearly defined, because it has numerous negative attributes, the term symbol seems to be of limited value. There is, however, one clear articulation of the term that I would like to discuss, for it provides yet another reason for our general avoidance of the term, or at least for its careful and restricted use. The term *symbol* is used by Charles Sanders Peirce to designate one class of signs in his complex, multilevel tripartite theory of signs, to which we owe much of this discussion. Peirce designated one tripartite class of signs as consisting of icon, index, and symbol.

These terms designate types of sign functional relationships. The *iconic* sign function is a relationship based on exemplification in some sense. The signal thus exhibits or exemplifies in some respect the sense in the mind of the user/perceiver. For example, a map exemplifies a territory, a picture exemplifies a landscape or an object, a diagram exemplifies structure or principles of operation. An *indexical* sign function is a relationship based on physical or spatial contiguity. The mind relates street signs to the contiguous street, pronouns to persons present or contiguous proper nouns. *Symbolic* sign functions, in Peirce's view, comprise the residual category, being neither iconic or indexical sign functions. More positively stated, they are sign functional relationships based on convention—that is, signal and sense are arbitrarily conjoined and yet this conjunction is held in common among sign users by means of convention. Natural languages are commonly used to illustrate this type of sign function, because it is easy to demonstrate that most words, as signals, have but an arbitrary connection with the sense to which they are related. Since the sound and spelling of the words for the same object or action in different languages often differ radically, this shows that the connection is at once arbitrary and based on convention. In Peircian terms then, symbol more accurately refers to the signs that comprise natural languages and less so to the majority of signs engaged in religious action. Since the study of religion has restricted itself heavily to the study of natural language materials and on the semantical-referential sense of the signs, on the basis of Peircian terms we might describe this as a study of symbols and symbolism. Rightly, then, it follows that since it is my wish to attempt to complement this emphasis, greater attention should be given to the types of signs that are not symbols—that is, to icons and indexes.

But even beyond this somewhat ironic point, the correlation of symbol with natural language is misleading, as should already be obvious. It is imperative to avoid the implication that a sign classification is a phenomenological category. I have offered several examples to show the error of this proclivity. Recall the Kiowa arrowmaker story. Certainly the words of the arrowmaker are "symbolic" in Peircian terms, and indeed it is the arrowmaker's knowledge of this that is the basis for and subject of his speech act. Kiowas share a convention of arbitrary correlations of sound sequences with senses. This is a language, and it is language that distinguishes the Kiowas from others. Nonetheless, while the arrowmaker's words are symbols, they are also indexes, for he places his speech in his exact temporal-spatial environment; he speaks to the intruder and to his wife in a way that calls for response, for actions in the present. In fact, were it not for the indexical functions of natural language, the arrowmaker could not act. He can shoot at the unknown person outside his lodge, confident that it is an enemy, only when he knows that his speech act has failed both as symbol and as index. But despite, indeed by virtue of, these failings the language act is ultimately successful in saving the lives of the arrowmaker and his family.

Because there is such a tendency to use the terms *icon, index,* and *symbol* as phenomenological classifications, perhaps these terms should not be used very extensively. There is a rough correlation between what has been designated the informative and the symbolic (in Peircian terms) and between the performative and the iconic and indexical, but the correlation is by no means exact; and while it is beneficial to be mindful of it, there should be no strict synonymity implied.

Interpretation and Validation. I am suggesting that the study of religion may focus on religious events and actions, yet as those events and actions are attested to by documents and other fixations. The interpretive task begins with a careful and thorough description of the action and its contextual domains. It requires the identification and illumination of the pragmatic and performative aspects of the actions and events. It requires a discernment of the purposes and motivations and the expected and actual effects achieved in the performance of the actions from a particular and specified point of view. Multiple points of view may, and often should, be considered. Interpretation also requires the consideration of the conventions, paradigms, and rules of use upon which the particular action is performed. This amounts to the discernment of the principles and potential meanings of the sign galaxies or portions thereof that are engaged by the set of actions. It requires a movement beyond immediate relevance to an examination of the importance of the actions to the history and society in which the set of actions occurs. I consider the interrelationship between relevance and importance, between event and tradition, between individual and community, between particular and universal, as the most illuminating dimension of interpreting religious actions.

I have, however, used words like *discern* and *consider* repeatedly in this description of what constitutes interpretation, and it is obvious that these are not precise terms. How does one discern purpose? How does one identify motivation? How does one consider interrelationships? I believe that there is no simple set of procedures for accomplishing these tasks, and certainly not for bringing all these together in a coherent interpretation. What these tasks require is experience and practice in performing them, the expenditure of considerable labor in describing and acquiring the data, and certain insight that may be enhanced by experience. Even this in no way guarantees making a good interpretation. In the end, an interpretation amounts to a statement that to the interpreter seems to make the most sense in light of all the data known and all the principles of interpretation. It amounts to one's best guess.

We need not dispair at this understanding of interpretation as one's best guess, for an interpretation, even a guess, need not be invalid. While there are not set and pat rules for making good interpretations, there are rules for testing the validity of interpretations.[12] Validity is tested by subjecting an interpretation to criticism. This involves the verification of the data and logic used, but finally the interpretation is judged primarily in terms of a probabilistic measure; that is, on how likely it is valid. Validation is not verification, and it depends upon judgments of peers engaged in a critical process. This means that there is an interdependence between the construction of and the criticism of interpretation. The interaction between these modes constitutes the process of acquiring experience in making interpretation and the process leading toward the acquisition of truth.

The Interpretive Cycle. Nearly every definition, theory, and principle considered in this chapter seems to be bound in the discussion of two terms, and these are often in opposition or tension. Humans are at once users and perceivers of signs. Religion is at once the creation of and the discovery of reality. Sign galaxies are at once the reservoir for all sign acts and the source of all sign acts. Signs are relationships formed in the minds of individuals, but signs are possible only through interaction among members of a community. Thus religious acts and religious sign galaxies, individuals and communities, are interdependent.

This dyadic interrelationship appears also in the principles of interpreting religious actions. I have argued that meaning and purpose, while contrasting and distinct, are interdependent, as are the fixation and reactivation of religious actions, the informative and performative aspects of signs, relevance and importance, the particular and the universal, and finally the construction and criticism of interpretations.

This may seem circular in reasoning, and indeed it is; but despite the common dismissal of an argument on the grounds of its circularity, this is not a vicious circle, and I believe that narrow-mindedness and dogmatism are avoidable only by such a position. It is also a way of attempting to avoid the obvious poverty of functionalism.[13] The approach I am suggesting is centered on the functioning of signs and also on the pragmatic and purposive character of signs. Logically, when pressed, this suggests that some need preexists the sign function; and since no need may be discerned apart from signs, no sign may ever occur, for there can be no need out of which it may arise. However, purpose is not prior to the sign but is integral to the formation of sign. It is one of the three necessary elements of the sign function, and it stands in the primary position within this tripartite structure.

There are also other shortcomings that are commonly noted for a high dependence on discerning signs in terms of use and purpose. A simple example may illustrate one of these. If the meaning of a sign is equated with the use it appears to serve, it can be argued that this may be misleading. For example, if I observe someone using a book to prop open a door or a journal to spank a naughty child, it might be argued that I would miss the importance and intended value of the book or journal: the messages borne by the words therein. Yet I would argue that the opposite is also true. For example, if one remains concerned with the Bible in terms only of its words, its messages, its authorship, and its literary value, without observing the pragmatic uses not only of those words but of the very book that contains the words, this too is missing at least some of its value. For example, the Bible, as a book, is used in courts of law and in inauguration ceremonies to confirm an oath. The Bible, as a book, has commonly been brandished by preachers and adored by parishioners none of whom could read a word in it. This simply indicates that a book, as anything perceptible, can be the signal portion of a sign function. But signs can be discerned only when one identifies a specific perspective and situation. Even then the intelligibility of the sign is not adequately known apart from the knowledge of the sign galaxy in which it occurs and to which it contributes.

This principle of circularity and interdependence characterizes a creative attitude toward the study of religion. It is not our theories or our data that lead us to the ability to comprehend and appreciate religion. It is the insight and the capacity for insight gained through the admittedly circular process of constructing theory to explain data and utilizing data to determine the adequacy of proposed theories; interpreting data in light of theory and definition, and constructing theory and definition in light of data and experience. The process of studying religion works on us as we work on it.

This brings us finally to the necessary third dimension of what heretofore has been presented as a dyadic structure. The third dimension is the initiating, mediating, and operative human presence—that is, the student of religion. The principles and methods discussed are for naught unless they respond to and arise from the peculiar needs for knowledge and truth brought by the human student of religion. Thus all of the interdependent pairs that have been presented may be conjoined meaningfully only in a triadic arrangement that includes the student of religion as the third part, as the primary of the three parts.

NOTES

1. Sam D. Gill, *Sacred Words: A Study of Navajo Religion and Prayer* (Westport, CT: Greenwood Press, 1981).
2. See above, "Prayer as Person: The Performative Force in Navajo Prayer Acts."
3. See Victor Turner, *The Forest of Symbols: Aspects of Ndembu Ritual* (Ithica: Cornell University Press, 1967), chap. 6, "Muchona the Hornet, Interpreter of Religion."
4. Jonathan Z. Smith, *Map Is Not Territory: Studies in the History of Religions* (Leiden: E. J. Brill, 1978), pp. 290-91.
5. N. Scott Momaday, "The Man Made of Words," in *Indian Voices: The First Convocation of American Indian Scholars* (San Francisco: The Indian Historian Press, 1970), pp. 49-62.
6. See Charles Sanders Peirce, *Collected Papers*, vols. 1–6 ed. C. Hartshorne and P. Weiss; vols. 7–8 ed. A. W. Burks (Cambridge: Harvard University Press, 1931–1958). Peirce's work is extremely difficult, and I have relied upon a number of others who have interpreted and restated his theory of signs, most notably, C. W. Morris. The distinction of Peircian theory of signs in contrast with that of Ferdinand de Saussure is clearly stated in the article of Milton Singer, "For a Semiotic Anthropology," in *Sight, Sound, and Sense*, ed. Thomas A. Sebeok (Bloomington: Indiana University Press, 1978), pp. 203-31, esp. pp. 211-21.
7. Purpose is, I believe, a way of indicating the third element of the sign that was termed *interpretant* by Peirce. For a discussion of this term see Milton Singer, "Signs of the Self: An Exploration in Semiotic Anthropology," *American Anthropologist* 82 (1980): 496-98.
8. The notion of sign galaxy and particularly the view that there are major organizing principles that make sign galaxies cohere may in some ways be contiguous with the discussion of similar ideas like Pepper's notion of "root metaphor," Victor Turner's notion of "dominant symbol," S. Ortner's "key symbols," and Mill's "master symbols."
9. This distinction is not a new one. Over a century ago, in their studies of language Ferdinand de Saussure and Louis Hjelmsle introduced a parallel distinction between language (*langue*) and speech (*parole*). This distinction is made more in the manner presented here by Paul Ricoeur in "The Model of the Text: Meaningful Action Considered as Text," *Social Research* 38 (1971): 529-62, esp. pp. 530-31.
10. In Ricoeur's article he chooses the former. Certainly that is a viable alternative, but it entirely eliminates action rather than restoring action its most distinctive attributes.

11. See esp. J. L. Austin, *How to Do Things with Words*, ed. J. O. Urmson and Marina Sbisa (Cambridge: Harvard University Press, 1975), and J. R. Searle, *Speech Acts* (Cambridge: Cambridge University Press, 1969). In religious studies some adaptations have been made to speech act theory in application to religion. See, e.g., Benjamin Ray, "Performative Utterances in African Ritual," *History of Religions* 13 (1973): 16-35, and Wade Wheelock, "A Taxonomy of the Mantras in the New- and Full-Moon Sacrifice," *History of Religions* 19 (1980): 349-69.

12. Eric D. Hirsch, Jr., *Validity in Interpretation* (New Haven: Yale University Press, 1967), p. 25.

13. For a full discussion of this problem see Hans H. Penner, "The Poverty of Functionalism," *History of Religions* 11 (1971): 91-97.

Good-bye Columbus:
An Afterword

In November of 1983 I met in Santa Fe with a number of persons interested in considering what preparations might lead to the appropriate celebration and commemoration of the five hundredth anniversary of the first voyage of Columbus to America. I presented remarks from which the following short essay is excerpted. The remarks are addressed primarily to the study and perceptions of Native American religions within the academic study of religion. Foolishly I had not accounted for the fact that the others present were almost exclusively anthropologists and archaeologists. The response to my remarks was shocking to me, for I learned that only one of twenty or so present was aware of the academic study of religion, and most considered my statement that the study of Native American religions has been ignored, has yet really to begin, to be so grossly in error as to be utterly silly. I had no luck, even by invoking the statistics on the number of departments of religion and scholars in the area, in clarifying my position. Since my effort for the last decade has been to help develop a new field of study within the academic study of religion, it now seems that a crucial issue is whether the academic study of religion stands in any way distinct from anthropology. Historically this has not been a significant issue because, I believe, there has been an agreement within the academic community about the limitations of these fields: it has hinged on the presence or absence of writing. However, in the last decade there has been an increasing movement by anthropologists into the study of literate societies with research interests expressed on many fronts. I fail to see much of a complementary movement by students of religion. This is, of course, the movement I am calling for in every essay in this volume. Obviously any current study of Native American religions must depend heavily on the archaeological,

173

ethnograph, linguistic, and ethnographic record and much of the theory developed by the anthropology of religion. Nonetheless, the study of Native American religions and the academic study of religion, I believe, may be mutually enriched, and in ways complementary to the various fields of anthropology. This has been a premise underlying the foregoing essays, and to bring the collection full circle, I think it appropriate to conclude with this essay.

In the journal of his 1492 voyage Columbus wrote the following about the religion of the peoples he called "los indios": "They should be good servants and very intelligent, for I have observed that they soon repeat anything that is said to them, and I believe that they would easily be made Christians, for they appear to me to have no religion." And in a letter he wrote shortly after his journal entry, he referred again to the religion of these people. His single sentence on the subject is preceded by his observations on fish and followed by a detailed description of trees. He wrote, "They have no religion and I think that they would be very quickly Christianized, for they have a very ready understanding."

Columbus understood religion as identical with Christianity. Given the world in which he lived, he could scarcely have had any other understanding. For him to have recognized anything that he would call religion would have been as unlikely as it would have been for him to have recognized that he was not charting a course to the eastern shores of Asia.

As a student of religion I find no fault with Columbus holding this view of religion; he scarcely had an alternative, yet I find it profoundly disturbing that the view expressed by Columbus regarding religion stands today almost without alteration. Indeed, we continue, like Columbus, to be more interested in the fish and trees than in people and their religions. In the half-millennium period since Columbus the social sciences and humanities have enjoyed major development. The academic study of religion came to life late within this period. It has grown rapidly, now having thousands of teachers and researchers in North America. The academic study of religion has developed its interests to include religious traditions throughout history and throughout the world in an effort to come to terms with religion as an important dimension of being human. Despite this development the field of study continues to ignore almost wholly the peoples native to the Americas. The well-established field known as American religion is essentially a study of the history of American Christianity. In large measure it is but a study of American Protestantism, for it has regularly ignored even the centuries of Catholic Christian presence in the American Southwest and in Central America prior to the Anglican settlement at Jamestown. Native Americans have never been included in American religious history except in the terms expressed by Columbus—that is, as prospective souls to enfold within Christianity.

I consider this situation to be intolerable, yet I do not believe that it can be rectified simply by expanding the current approach of the academic study of religion to include these cultures. It is quite clear that this exclusion of Native Americans from the academic study of religion is symptomatic of much more deeply seated biases that are inseparable from many of the perspectives that have shaped the humanities and social sciences. The exclusion is rooted in the very character of Western intellectual history and is especially clear in the American academic understanding of religion. Thus, rectification will require fundamental revision.

Since the voyages of Columbus are inextricably connected with this matter, perhaps the upcoming celebration of the five hundredth anniversary of his first voyage may serve as a goal toward advancing this process of revision. Let me outline some elements that I believe must be included. America exists for us not because Columbus discovered it, especially not in the style described in Morrison's famous biography: "Never again may mortal men hope to recapture the amazement, the wonder, the delight of those October days in 1492 when the New World gracefully yielded her virginity to the conquering Castilins." Rather, as Edmundo O'Gorman has shown in his book *The Invention of America*, America exists for us as "America" because, after Columbus' death some Europeans began to recognize the incongruity between the observations of Columbus and other travelers and what was known about the world at the time. The beginning of a resolution to this incongruity was the invention of the idea of a "new world." They called it America. American history may be seen as the working out over time of the identity of this idea, expressed through images of the landscape and through actions of peoples within this landscape. I believe that

O'Gorman's work forces us to revise our understanding not only of America and American history, but of historical processes and the writing of history. American history has been made and written in the process of responding to and resolving the incongruities that have existed between our experience in America and the expectations that stem from our images of America.

In this light we may discern the character and history of the encounter with the peoples native to the Americas. It was the recognition and experience of incongruity that gave rise to the invention of America. But in the time of Columbus no such incongruity was recognized between the images and expectations held for "los indios" and the actual peoples encountered. More importantly, no such incongruity has ever been recognized. As Columbus believed that he had found a trade route to Asia, we have persisted in the belief that we know these Indians. The significance of the voyages of Columbus arose only when it was recognized that the observations he made did not correspond to the maps he was using. Yet we have persisted, erroneously I think, in upholding with confidence our belief that the Indians we observe are the ones described in our guides. American history documents this fact. Government policy has always assumed that "we" know what "they" want and need even more than they do, even when they express alternatives views. At best it has been a policy of paternalism, but commonly even this parental dimension has been supplanted by one of termination and displacement to meet the exigencies of the advancement of civilization and Christianity. The academic consideration of native peoples has been done primarily by anthropologists whose traditional purview has been those we have termed "primitive peoples"; this means, to unpack the prejudice of the term, peoples whose cultures were disappearing in the face of the more modern, more advanced societies. We have known the peoples native to the Americas variously as "noble savages" and as "dirty dogs." The history of our encounter with them as actual peoples has been almost wholly shaped by the terms of these images, whether it be to attempt to make them farmers on small plots of land like European-American settlers, to make them Christians to save them from their heathen ways, to use them to sell ourselves margarine by projecting images of the purity and healthfulness of a corn-growing Indian maiden, or to use them as counterimages with which to whip ourselves for polluting the earth.

To put it in terms of the quincentenary, as far as comprehending Native American cultures and especially the religious dimensions of these many complex cultures, I believe that we are still in the boat with Columbus. We have yet to perceive the radical incongruities that exist between what we believe that we know about them and what and who they really are. We, like Columbus before us, inevitably find what we set out to find, see what we want to see. At least in the academic study of religion we, like Columbus before us, express through our actions if not through clear statement that Native Americans have no religion. We remain deaf to their insistence that we have not understood them, that we have not seen them, that our studies radically transform, even violate, them.

To me, a major goal for the Columbian quincentenary should be to begin to recognize and to attempt to come to terms with this fundamental incongruity. In the academic study of religion this would require the initiation of the academic study of Native Amrican religions. This cannot be done in any way that is academically respectable without also rethinking fundamental aspects of the entire field of study.

As a quincentenary goal in the area of Native American studies I would hope that we might first recognize the incongruities that have existed for nearly five hundred years in our envisioning and encountering the peoples native to the Americas, and that this recognition might open a greater sensitivity and respect as well as a revisioning and renewal widely experienced in the academic study of religion and perhaps other academic fields. My highest hope would be that not only would we come to see and hear more fully and more accurately, but that our new vision would initiate a new era in which a fuller human encounter characterized by openness and dignity might take place among all peoples of America. In short, my quincentenary hope would be that after five hundred years we might finally step off the boat.

Bibliography

Aberle, David F. "The Navajo Singer's 'Fee': Payment or Prestation?" In *Studies in Southwestern Ethnolinguistics: Meaning and History in the Languages of the American Southwest,* edited by Dell H. Hymes and William E. Bittle, 15-32. The Hague: Mouton, 1967.

Austin, J. L. *How to Do Things with Words,* 2d ed., edited by J. O. Urmson and Marina Sbisa. Cambridge: Harvard University Press, 1975.

Baraku, Amiri Imamu [LeRoi Jones]. "Hunting Is Not Those Heads on the Wall." In *Home: Social Essays,* 173-78. New York: Morrow, 1972.

Bellow, Saul. *Mr. Sammler's Planet.* New York: Viking Press, 1969.

Brasser, Ted. "North American Indian Art for TM." In *The Religious Character of Native American Humanities,* edited by Sam Gill, 126-43. Tempe: Department of Religious Studies, Arizona State University, 1977.

Carpenter, Edmund. *Eskimo Realities.* New York: Holt, Rinehart & Winston, 1973.

Davis, William H. "Synthetic Knowledge as 'Abduction'." *Southern Journal of Philosophy,* Spring 1970; 37-43.

Deloria, Vine, Jr. *Custer Died for Your Sins: An Indian Manifesto.* New York: Avon, 1969.

Dieterich, Albrecht. *Mutter Erde: Ein Versuch über Volksreligion.* Berlin-Leipzig, 1905.

Earle, E., and E.A. Kinnard. *Hopi Kachina.* New York: J.J. Augustin, 1938.

Eggan, Dorothy. "The General Problem of Hopi Adjustment." *American Anthropologist* 45 (1943): 357-73.

Fann, K.T. *Peirce's Theory of Abduction.* The Hague: Martinus Nijhoff, 1970.

Fergusson, Erna. *Dancing Gods: Indian Ceremonials of New Mexico and Arizona.* Albuquerque: University of New Mexico Press, 1957.

Fewkes, J. Walter. *Ancestor Worship of the Hopi Indians.* Smithsonian Annual Report for 1921. Washington, D.C., 1923.

_____. "On Certain Personages Who Appear in a Tusayan Ceremonial." *American Anthropologist* 7(1894): 32-53.

_____. *Tusayan Kachinas*. Bureau of American Ethnology, 15th Annual Report. Washington, D.C., 1897.

Finnegan, Ruth. "How to Do Things with Words: Performative Utterances among the Limba of Sierra Leone." *Man*, n.s. 4 (1969): 537-52.

Gill, Sam D. *Beyond "the Primitive": The Religions of Nonliterate Peoples.* Englewood Cliffs, NJ: Prentice-Hall, 1982.

_____. *Mother Earth: An American Story.* Chicago: The University of Chicago Press, 1987.

_____. *Native American Religions: An Introduction.* Belmont, CA: Wadsworth Publishing Company, 1982.

_____. *Native American Traditions: Sources and Interpretations.* Belmont, CA: Wadsworth Publishing Company, 1983.

_____. "Prayer." *The Encyclopedia of Religion.* New York: Macmillan, 1986.

_____. *Sacred Words: A Study of Navajo Religion and Prayer.* Westport, CT: Greenwood Press, 1981.

_____. *Songs of Life: An Introduction to Navajo Religious Culture.* Leiden: E.J. Brill, 1979.

Goody, Jack. *The Domestication of the Savage Mind.* London: Oxford University Press, 1965.

Gossen, Gary H. "Language as Ritual Substance." In *Language in Religious Practice.* Edited by William J. Samarin, 40-62. Rowley, MA: Newbury House, 1976.

Gray, Louis. "Hopi." In *Encyclopedia of Religion and Ethics*, edited by James Hastings, 6: 783-89. New York: Scribner's, 1920.

Green, Jesse. *Zuñi: Selected Writings of Frank Hamilton Cushing.* Lincoln: Unversity of Nebraska Press, 1979.

Haile, Berard, O.F.M. *Origin Legend of the Navaho Enemy Way.* New Haven: Yale University Publications in Anthropology 17, 1938.

_____. "Soul Concepts of the Navaho." *Annali Lateranesi* 7 (1943): 59-94.

Hallowell, A.I. "Ojibwa Ontology, Behavior, and World View." In *Culture in History: Essays in Honor of Paul Radin*, edited by Stanley Diamond, 18-52. New York: Columbia Unversity Press, 1960.

Hanson, Norwood R. *Patterns of Discovery: An Inquiry into the Conceptual Foundations of Science.* Cambridge: Cambridge University Press, 1965.

Hieb, Louis. "Meaning and Mismeaning: Toward an Understanding of the Ritual Clown." In *New Perspectives on the Pueblos*, edited by Alfonso Ortiz, 163-95. Albuquerque: University of New Mexico Press, 1972.

Hirsch, Eric D., Jr. *Validity in Interpretation.* New Haven: Yale University Press, 1967.

Holm, Bill, and Bill Reid. *Indian Art of the Northwest Coast: A Dialogue on Craftsmanship and Aesthetics.* Seattle: University of Washington Press, 1975.

Howitt, A.W. *The Native Tribes of South-East Australia.* London: Macmillan, 1904.

Huggins, E.L. "Smohalla, the Prophet of Priest Rapids." *Overland Monthly.* San Francisco, 2d Ser., 17 no. 98, Jan.-June, 1891.

Hymes, Dell. "The Americanist Tradition." In *American Indian Languages and American Linguistics,* edited by Wallace L. Chafe, 11-28. Lisse: The Peter de Ridder Press, 1976.

"Indian Speeches Delivered by Farmer's Brother and Red Jacket, Two Seneca Chiefs." Prepared by James D. Bemis. Canandaigua, NY, 1809.

James, William. *The Varieties of Religious Experience.* New York: Collier, 1962. First published 1902.

Jenness, Diamond. "The Carrier Indians of Bulkley River." Bureau of American Ethnology Bulletin no. 133. Washington, D.C., 1943.

Langer, Suzanne K. *Philosophy in a New Key.* Cambridge: Harvard University Press, 1942.

Lowie, Robert H. *Primitive Religion.* New York: Liveright, 1970. First published 1924.

MacMurray, J.W. "The 'Dreamers' of the Columbia River Valley, in Washington Territory." *Transactions of the Albany Institute.* Albany, 1887.

Marett, R.R. *The Threshold of Religion,* 2d. ed. London, 1914.

Matthews, R. H. "The Būrbūng of the Wiradthuri Tribes." *Journal of the Anthropological Institute of Great Britain and Ireland* 25 (1896): 295-317.

Matthews, Washington. "Mythic Dry-Paintings of the Navajos." *American Naturalist* 19 (1885): 931-39.

————. *Night Chant, a Navajo Ceremony.* New York: American Museum of Natural History, Memoirs vol. 6, 1902.

Means, Russell. "Fighting Words on the Future of the Earth." *Mother Jones,* Dec. 1980; pp. 22-38.

Momaday, N. Scott. "The Man Made of Words." In *Indian Voices: The First Convocation of American Indian Scholars,* 49-62. San Francisco: The Indian Historian Press, 1970.

Mooney, James. *The Ghost Dance Religion and the Sioux Outbreak of 1890.* Bureau of American Ethnology, 14th Annual Report. Washington, D.C., 1896.

Neihardt, John. *Black Elk Speaks.* New York: Pocket Books, 1972. First published 1932.

Niane, D.T. *Sundiata: An Epic of Old Mali*. London: Longmans, 1965.

O'Gorman, Edmundo. *The Invention of America*. Bloomington: Indiana University Press, 1961.

O'Kane, Walter C. *Sun in Sky*. Norman: University of Oklahoma Press, 1950.

Parsons, Elsie C. *A Pueblo Indian Journal*. Menesha, WI: American Anthropological Association, Memoirs no. 2, 1925.

––––––. *Pueblo Indian Religion*. 2 vols. Chicago: The University of Chicago Press, 1939.

Peek, Philip M. "The Power of Words in African Verbal Arts." *Journal of American Folklore* 94 (1981): 19-43.

Peirce, Charles Sanders. *Collected Papers*. Vols. 1-6, edited by C. Hartshorne and P. Weiss; Vols. 7-8, edited by A.W. Burks. Cambridge: Harvard University Press, 1931-1958.

––––––. "Guessing." *The Hound and the Horn* 2 (1929): 267-82.

Penner, Hans H. "The Poverty of Functionalism." *History of Religions* 11 (1971): 91-97.

Radin, Paul. *Primitive Religion*. New York: Dover, 1957. First published 1937.

Rasmussen, Knud. *The People of the Polar North: A Record*. London: Kegan Paul, Trench, Trubner & Co., 1908.

Ravenhill, Philip L. "Religious Utterances and the Theory of Speech Acts." In *Language in Religious Practice*, edited by William J. Samarin, 26-39. Rowley, MA: Newbury House, 1976.

Ray, Benjamin. "Performative Utterances in African Ritual." *History of Religions* 13 (1973): 16-35.

Reichard, Gladys. *Prayer: The Compulsive Word*. New York: J.J. Augustin, 1944.

Ricoeur, Paul. "The Model of the Text: Meaningful Action Considered as Text." *Social Research* 38 (1971): 529-62.

Schoolcraft, Henry Rowe. *Travels in the Central Portions of the Mississippi Valley: Comprising Observations on Its Minerals, Geography, Internal Resources, Aboriginal Population*. Performed under the Sanction of Government in the year 1821. New York: Collins & Hanney, 1825.

Searle, John R. *Speech Acts*. Cambridge: Cambridge University Press, 1969.

Sebeok, Thomas A. "One, Two, Three Spells U B E R T Y (in lieu of an introduction)." In *The Sign of Three: Dupin, Holmes, Peirce*, edited by Umberto Eco and Thomas A. Sebeok, 1-9. Bloomington: Indiana University Press, 1983.

Sekaquaptewa, Emory. "Hopi Ceremonies." In *Seeing with a Native Eye*, edited by Walter H. Capps, 35-43. New York: Harper & Row, 1976.

Silverstein, Michael. "Metaforces of Power in Traditional Oratory." A lecture delivered at Yale and the University of Chicago, spring, 1981.

Singer, Milton. "For a Semiotic Anthropology." In *Sight, Sound, and Sense*, edited by Thomas A. Sebeok, 203-31. Bloomington: Indiana University Press, 1978.

————. "Signs of the Self: An Exploration in Semiotic Anthropology." *American Anthropologist* 82 (1980): 485-507.

Smith, Jonathan Z. *Map Is Not Territory: Studies in the History of Religions.* Leiden: E. J. Brill, 1978.

————. "A Pearl of Great Price and a Cargo of Yams: A Study in Situational Incongruity." In *Imagining Religion: From Babylon to Jamestown*, 90-101. Chicago: The Unversity of Chicago Press, 1982.

Stephen, Alexander M. *Hopi Journal of Alexander M. Stephen*, edited by Elsie C. Parsons. New York: Columbia University Press, 1936.

Stevenson, James. *Ceremonial of Hasjelti Dailjis and Mythical Sand Painting of the Navajo Indians.* Bureau of American Ethnology, 8th Annual Report. Washington, D.C., 1891.

Steward, Julian H. "Notes on Hopi Ceremonies in Their Initiatory Form." *American Anthropologist* 33 (1931): 56-79.

Talayesva, Don C. *Sun Chief: An Autobiography of a Hopi Indian.* Edited by Leo W. Simmons. New Haven: Yale University Press, 1942.

Tambiah, Stanley J. "Form and Meaning of Magical Acts: A Point of View." In *Modes of Thought*, edited by Robin Horton and Ruth Finnegan, 199-229. London: Faber & Faber, 1973.

————. "The Magical Power of Words." *Man*, n.s. 3 (1968): 177-208.

Tedlock, Dennis. "From Prayer to Reprimand." In *Language in Religious Practice*, edited by William J. Samarin, 72-83. Rowley, MA: Newbury House, 1976.

————. "Verbal Art." In *Handbook of North American Indians*, William C. Sturtevant, general editor, vol. 1, chap. 50, Washington. D. C.: Smithsonian Institution, in press.

Thompson, Robert. *African Art in Motion.* Berkeley and Los Angeles: University of California Press, 1974.

Titiev, Mischa. *Old Oraibi: A Study of the Hopi Indians of Third Mesa.* Cambridge: Paper of the Peabody Museum of American Archaeology and Ethnology, vol. 12, no. 1, 1944.

————. *The Hopi Indians of Old Oraibi: Change and Continuity.* Ann Arbor: University of Michigan Press, 1972.

Turner, Victor. *Chihamba the White Spirit: A Ritual Drama of the Ndembu.* Rhodes-Livingstone Paper no. 33. New York: Humanities Press, 1962.

_____. *The Forest of Symbols: Aspects of Ndembu Ritual.* Ithaca: Cornell University Press, 1967.

Tylor, Edward B. *Primitive Culture.* London: John Murray, 1873.

Underhill, Ruth. *The Navajos.* Norman: University of Oklahoma Press, 1956.

_____. *Singing for Power: The Song Magic of the Papago Indians of Southern Arizona.* Berkeley and Los Angeles: University of California Press, 1968.

van der Leeuw, G. *Religion in Essence and Manifestation.* New York: Harper & Row, 1963.

van Gennep, Arnold. *Rites of Passage.* Chicago: The University of Chicago Press, 1901.

Voth, H. R. *The Oraibi Powamu Ceremony.* Chicago: Field Columbian Museum Publication 61, Anthropological Series, vol. 3, no. 2, 1901.

Wallace, A. F. C. "New Religions Among the Delaware Indians, 1600–1900." *Southwest Journal of Anthropology* 12, no. 1 (1956): 1-21.

Waters, Frank. *The Book of the Hopi.* New York: Viking Press, 1963.

Watts, Alan W. *The Two Hands of God: The Myths of Polarity.* New York: Braziller, 1963.

Wheelock, Wade. "A Taxonomy of the Mantras in the New- and Full-Moon Sacrifice." *History of Religions* 19(1980): 349-69.

Witherspoon, Gary. *Language and Art in the Navajo Universe.* Ann Arbor: University of Michigan Press, 1977.

Worsley, Peter. *The Trumpet Shall Sound,* rev. ed. New York: Schocken, 1968.

Wyman, Leland C. *Beautyway, a Navaho Ceremonial.* New York: Pantheon, 1975.

_____. *Blessingway.* Tucson: University of Arizona Press, 1970.

_____. *The Windways of the Navaho.* Colorado Springs: Taylor Museum of Colorado Springs Fine Arts, 1962.

Young, Robert W., and William Morgan. *The Navajo Language.* Salt Lake City: Deseret Book Co., 1972.

Index

Abduction (abductive inference), 9–15, 151
Aberle, David, 29
Action: religion as, 8, 9, 113, 120–21, 123–24, 126, 135, 137, 140, 141, 149–57; interpretation of religious action, 158–70. *See also* Prayer
Africa: Ndembu initiation, 68–69; storyteller on literacy, 133–34
African art, 46 n.6
Algonkian: effigy pipe, 41
America: discovery/invention of, 175–76
American religion: exclusion of Native American religions, 175
Anthropology: compared to academic study of religion, 174; conceptions of Native Americans, 176
Art, 37–45
Austin, J. L., 113, 118–20, 124, 128 n.12, 163

Baraku, Amiri Imamu [LeRoi Jones], 44
Bean Dance (Hopi Pomamu), 32–34, 58–66
Bellow, Saul, 25
Bible (Christian), 143, 144, 170
Black Elk, 35–36
Blackening rite (Navajo), 104–5, 106, 109
Blessingway (Navajo ceremonial), 19, 21, 22, 23
Book Indian (literate Indian), 133
Brasser, Ted, 41
Bullroarer, 67–68

Carpenter, Edmund, 45
Carrier (tribe in British Columbia), 131

Changing Woman (Navajo), 22–23
Chief Joseph (Nez Perce), 81
Christianity: initiation structure in scripture, 71–72; elements in Smohalla's creation story, 82; importance in study of Native American religions, 174–75; Christianization of Indians, 174–76
Clowns: Hopi, 34; Zuni, 75 n.17
Columbus, Christopher, 173–77
Conquest/dominance: shaping categories of study of Native Americans, 130–34, 136–39
Cosmological patterns, 24
Cram, The Reverend Mr. (missionary), 131–32
Creation/Creativity: 17–25, 29, 31, 38, 44, 85, 98, 101, 106, 109, 119, 121, 126, 134–35, 141
Creation stories: general, 18; Navajo, 18–19, 24, 29; Papago, 17; told by Smohalla, 82–83
Criticism, 168–69
Crow-Wing (Hopi), 73 n.8
Cushing, Frank Hamilton, 89–90, 92, 130

Dakota (Sioux), 35–36
Delaware prophet (Neolin), 143
Deloria, Vine, Jr., 132, 134
Dieterich, Albrecht, 86
Discovery, pattern of, 12
Disenchantment, 35, 58–72
Dreamers, 88 n.3 and n.4. *See also* Smohalla.

Eggan, Dorothy, 62–63
Eggan, Fred, 63

Eliade, Mircea, 87
Emetic rite (Navajo), 100–1, 108
Empty Tomb (Christian), 71–72
Enemyway (Navajo ceremonial),
   99–110
Eskimo, 45. *See also* Inuit

Functionalism, avoiding poverty of,
   169–70

Ghost Dance (1890), 86
Goody, Jack, 139
Gospels (Christian scripture), 71–72
Gossen, Gary, 94
Gray, Louis, 61–62
Guardian spirit, 41–42

Hanson, Norwood R., 12
Harrison, William Henry, 77–80
Health and healing, 38–40, 41, 47–57,
   114, 121, 122–26
Heiler, Frederick, 90, 92
History: conceptions of, 76–88 (esp.
   84), 175–76
Holybook (scripture), 129, 138, 142,
   143–45
Holyway (Navajo Ceremonial way),
   114–24
Hopi, 3–4, 7, 32–35, 42–43, 58–66
House: Navajo blessing of, 19–20
Hultkrantz, Ake, 87
Humankind: definition of, 153–54
Hypothesis, construction of (abduc-
   tion), 9–15

Icon (class of signs), 166–67
Incongruity, 175–77
Index (class of signs), 166–67
Indian (term), 87
Infelicities: doctrine of in Navajo
   prayer, 124–25
Informative function, 140, 141, 161–63
Initiation: Hopi, 32–35, 58–66;
   Wiradthuri (Australia), 67–68;
   Ndembu (Africa), 68–69; Christian,
   71–72; use of masks, 42–43
Interpretant, 171 n.7
Interpretation: of religious action,
   158–70; compared to understanding,
   158–59; validation of, 167–68; pro-
   cess described, 167–68; interpretive
   cycle, 169–70
Inuit, 132

Iroquois, 41

Jesus, 71–72, 143

Kachina (Hopi figure), 3–4, 32–35,
   42–43, 58–66
Kachina Society (Hopi), 32
Kiowa: arrowmaker story, 153–54, 167

Langer, Susanne, 93
Language: power of, 18
Literacy, 129, 130, 132–45 (esp.
   138–39)
Long Life and Happiness (Navajo
   figures and concept), 106, 107, 109,
   121
Lowie, Robert, 93

MacMurray, J. W., 82, 85
Mark (Gospel), 71–72
Mask, 4, 32–33, 42–44, 48–49, 59,
   61–66
Matthews, Washington, 37, 50
Mead, Margaret, 33
Meaning, 160–67
Means, Russell (Lakota), 133–35, 139
Medicine bundle, 21, 22–23, 29
Missionization (Christian) of Indians,
   131–32, 134
Momaday, N. Scott, 18, 153–54
Mooney, James, 86
Morris, Charles W., 171 n.6
Mother Earth/Motherhood of the earth,
   85–87
Mountain soil bundle (Navajo ritual
   object), 22–23
Muchona (Ndembu African), 68, 69,
   149
Myth, 76, 84, 139. *See also* Story and
   Creation stories

Native American religions: academic
   study of, 5–9, 11–12, 15, 151
Nature, 24
Navajo: Blessingway (a ceremonial),
   19, 21; ceremonialism, 23, 28–29,
   114; creation, 18–19, 29; life, conception of, 119; house blessing,
   19–20; medicine bundle, 19, 22–23,
   29; prayer, 93–110 (Enemyway
   prayer, 98–110), 113–126 (Navajo
   Windway Prayer, 115–24), prayer,
   study of, 147–51, 162–63; sand
   painting, 21, 30, 37–40, 47–57;

social relationships, 27–29, 31, 37;
elder's statement on forgetting story,
136
Ndembu (Africa): initiation, 68–69
Neihardt, John, 35–36
Nightway (Navajo ceremonial), 47–57
Niman (Hopi ceremonial), 3–4
Nonliteracy (exclusive orality), 5, 8,
129–45
Northwest Coast art, 46 n.7

Oglala (Sioux), 35–36
O'Gorman, Edmundo, 175–76

Papago, 17–18
Papua (Papua-New Guinea), 143
Parsons, Elsie C., 60
Peirce, Charles Sanders, 9–13, 15, 155,
166–67
Performance: approach to study of reli-
gion, 7, 9; masking, 35, 43–44;
prayer, 90, 93, 94, 95, 96–110,
113–26 (esp. 123–26), 149–50; sand
painting (Navajo), 30–32, 38–39;
song, 18; other, 18, 25, 35, 36, 130,
137, 140–45, 151, 161, 163, 167–68
Performative force, 107
Performative function, 140, 141,
142–45, 161–63, 167
Performative utterance, 113, 118–26
Person: Navajo prayer as, 113–26;
Native American concepts of, 128
n.13
Perspective: visual, 38–45, 55–56
Pipe: effigy, 41–42
Popular religion, 142
Powamu (Hopi ceremonial), 58–66
Powamu Society (Hopi), 32
Pragmatic: aspects of prayer, 113, 119,
122–26; aspects of sign functions,
161–63, 169–70
Prayer: Navajo, 24, 113–26; Navajo
creation prayer, 21; Navajo
Enemyway prayer, 98–110; Navajo
Nightway prayer, 20–21, 55; Navajo
walk-in-beauty prayer, 22; Navajo
Windway prayer, 115–26; Reichard's
study of, 92–94; study of, 89–95,
110–11, 147–51, 162–63; Tylor's
study of, 90–92
Prayer act, 113, 122–26

Prayer stick and offering ritual (Navajo), 115–26
Prophetic movements in North
America, 143
Purpose: aspect of sign function, 156;
related to meaning, 160–61; informa-
tive/performative, 161–63; relevance, 163; in interpretive process,
167; in avoiding functionalism,
169–70; compared to Peirce's "interpretant", 171 n.7

Radin, Paul, 93
Rasmussen, Knud, 132
Ravenhill, Philip, 94
Red Jacket (Seneca), 131–32, 134
Reichard, Gladys, 92–94, 113
Religion: academic study of, 5–9,
11–12, 13, 15, 136–37, 148, 150,
151–52, 158, 163–64, 166, 169–70,
173–77; as action, 8, 157–70; defini-
tion of, 8, 9, 137–43, 150–53
Ricoeur, Paul, 171 n.9 and n.10
Rites of passage: Hopi, 32–35, 58–66;
Ndembu (Africa), 68–69; Wiradthuri
(Australia), 67–68
Ritual. See Creation/Creativity, Prayer,
Rites of passage, Sand painting

Sahaptin, 87. See also Smohalla
Sand painting (Navajo), 21, 30–32,
37–40, 47–57
Schoolcraft, Henry Rowe, 78–79
Sekaquaptewa, Emory (Hopi), 43, 74
n.15
Self-directed orientation in design, 41
Seneca, 131–32
Shaman: use of effigy pipe, 41
Shawnee, 87. See also Tecumseh
Sign or Sign function, 153–70; in definition of humankind, 153–54;
defined, 154–56; related to sign galaxy, 157; as religious action, 157,
159; meaning of, 160–62; compared
to symbol, 164–67; types of, 166; in
interpretation, 166–70
Sign galaxy, 156; compared to sign
function, 157–58; and religious
action, 159–60; universality, 163; in
interpretation, 168, 170
Silverstein, Michael, 146 n.9

Singer, Milton (on Peirce and de Saus-
sure), 171 n.6
Sioux, 35–36, 41
Smith, Jonathan Z., 12
Smohalla (Wanapum), 81–83, 84, 85,
86, 132–33
Socrates, 135
Song, 18, 19, 20, 23, 24, 114. *See also*
Prayer
Soyoko (Hopi ritual), 42–43
Speech act, 153–54. *See also* Prayer
and Song
Speech and thought (Navajo concept),
121. *See also* Long Life and Happi-
ness
Stephen, Alexander M., 59–61
Steward, Julian, 73 n.1 and n.8
Story, 24, 76–88, 138–39; Kiowa
arrowmaker story, 153–54; Navajo
stories, 18–24, 29, 31, 38, 49–52,
99, 109, 115, 117–18, 121, 136;
Papago creation story, 17
Structural study of Navajo prayer,
93–94, 98–110, 113, 116–24,
147–51
Surprise: in creating hypotheses, 12–15
Symbol, 155, 160–61, 164–67
Symbolic approach to study of prayer,
93–94

Talayesve, Don (Hopi), 42–43, 62, 66
Tambiah, Stanley J., 94
Tecumseh (Shawnee), 77–81, 83, 84,
85, 86

Tedlock, Dennis, 94
Text: in academic study of religion,
8–9, 137–40, 141, 148–50
Tippecanoe (battle), 79
Titiev, Mischa, 63–64
Tobacco, 41–42
Torah scrolls, 144
Turner, Victor, 68–69, 71, 94, 149
Tylor, Edward B., 86, 90–92, 97, 110

Understanding: compared to interpretation, 158–59
Unraveling rite (Navajo), 104, 106,
108, 109

Vailala Madness (Papua-New Guinea),
143
van der Leeuw, G., 93
Voth, Heinrick, 60–61

War of 1812, 80
Waters, Frank, 73 n.8
Whirling Logs sand painting (Navajo),
47–57 (story, 50–52)
White Bear (Hopi), 73 n.8
White Singer, Doc (Navajo), 147–48,
150
Wiradthuri (Australia), 67–68
Word: power of, 18. *See also* Prayer
and Story
World view, 24
Writing, 173. *See also* Literacy and
Nonliteracy

Zuni, 75 n.17, 89–90, 92, 130, 134